# The Queen's Gambol

## *Chess and Women's*

## *Power*

**ART DIRECTOR: CHRISTOPHER CUFF**
**COVER DESIGN: KATE SILK**
Silk.kate@yahoo.com

Publisher:  **DPC** DPCarr Press
Subsidiary of CarrPub

# DEDICATION

Janina Ronsevic is ingenious at ferreting out avenues for the dissemination of important matters. Her years spent in the company of celebrities polished her ingenuity, and enhanced her innate good taste and unfailing good humor. The world is a better place with Janina here.

# FROM ROCK TO REAL

# CONTENTS

# ACKNOWLEDGMENTS

The Queen's Gambol would not be as much fun without the antics of the cartoon Queen. Christopher Cuff discovered her and guided her though her transition from inert matter to the Dancing Queen she became. Casey Donahue and Regina Jagielski taught the Chess Queen to Gambol. Then, Patricia Donahue, took the Queen seriously, and deposited her into context where she sets a lively pace for the surprising facts to follow. Aaron Tupper challenged her gambol across the Chess Board with intriguing chess puzzles.

# PREFACE
# Two Paths Converge

The story of women's progress towards equality was rarely pleasant; it was and can yet remain mostly tedious and often dangerous. Only in the game of Chess it happened that the Queen, though derided as "Mad," evolved into a truly liberated lady, more than equal. We can join her as she debuts, and proceeds to gambol through the centuries. She's sometimes the Black Queen and sometimes the White, but she's always the most powerful and play-full piece on the board.

Let's assume that those who call the game of chess "immortal" are correct. If so, then we might conjecture that the original 6th century clay blob that sat next to the king clay blob had within it the blueprint of the unshackled woman extant today. Let's pick up her story there, shapeless in form, but not in intent. We'll follow her, the very first Chess Queen, cheering her successes, and suffering her obstacles as our little avatar's life mirrors the blossoming of women's rights.

Women's ultimate reckoning is a matter of common sense; like suffrage, it had to happen. But can we look at it through a parallel lens so that the struggles of centuries ultimately prove to be instructive? The freedom of women continues to grow; it is irrepressible like the slow growth and unfolding of a lotus flower. Competing forces can't forever repress what is natural.

So, with our 21st Century eyes, we'll look backwards to move forwards. The Chess Queen was often tripped up along the way. Maybe her stumbles and triumphs will offer practical guidance for today's women navigating boldly in a man's world. **Let's watch as** alongside each other, the Queen of Chess and the women of persistent intent create their own destiny.

# *ENTER...THE CHESS QUEEN*

1

# THE CHESS QUEEN GAMBOLS ONTO THE STAGE

The Chess Queen burst onto the scene with style, her opening gambit danced with *gambetto*, Italian for "kicking up of the heels." But, in fact, she had been waiting in the wings for a very long time. She's wasn't young when she was finally liberated, and she's about 1100 years old now, if you don't count her transgender time as a vizier, ( the king's general and advisor) in 6th Century India.

Back then, as the king's sidekick, a.k.a. the vizier, the once and future Queen's sole purpose was to defend the king. This single reason for being had smothered the essence and grit of the superbly agile and resourceful game piece she would become. Eventually she would evolve into the most powerful figure in the immortal game of chess. Well enough, but ironically, her centuries long rise to power was faster than the struggle that actual women waged for their rightful voice in democracy. Some women, sadly, are still denied basic rights even today.

It was the real-life 15th Century chess playing European Queens, especially Isabella of Aragon, who modelled the liberated Chess Queen. Because she was powerful and bold, and could not be constrained, Isabella became the avatar for the new game of Chess, the "Mad Queen's Chess." The innovators imbued their Chess Queens with audacious options. These game Queen complements of the European Queens could dart clear across the board, maybe checking the king or taking out a bishop or a knight or any other piece in their way.

The Chess Queen's "evolution" is a roadmap for women's evolution, for the gradual acceptance of women's innate power. Those talents were buried in culture and prejudice, or servitude, but could not be contained permanently. In America, women reflected the Chess Queens' purpose in the 1848 Seneca Falls Convention when they liberated women with the Declaration of Rights and Sentiments for Women signed by 68 women and 32 men. It was Frederick Douglass, a former slave, whose attendance at the convention and support of the Declaration helped to pass the resolution. Another slave, Harriet Tubman, escaped and rose to the honorary title of "Conductor" on the Underground Railroad. Like the lowliest chess pieces, the pawns, these and other brave former slaves were able to penetrate the offensive white pieces and prevail.

Women throughout recorded time, until recent centuries, were almost universally viewed as subservient to men. Ginger Rogers danced backwards, wearing high heels. Fred Astaire got the praise, consensus being that she was a worthy partner, a good facilitator of his genius. That Dancing Queen's function was to showcase the King. Sound familiar? Think docile First Ladies with a "cause?"

There always were women who rose to prominence, daring to act beyond their assigned moves. Like the Chess Queen, they might have moved to target the church (bishop), or the president (king) to criticize or to replace those "pieces." Katherine Jefferts Schori took over as the first female Presiding Bishop of the Episcopal Church. Victoria Woodhull, made two attempts to become the United States President, running in 1884 and 1886. Hillary Clinton was the Electoral College away from President in 2016. General Maryanne Miller, the only female Four Star General becomes the knight, and in 2021 144 women storm the castle, the US Congress. Just like the unfettered Chess Queen, the 21st Century woman is largely free to travel as she would.

But the chess board still confines the Queen into its 64 squares. No matter her prowess, the Chess Queen cannot surpass these boundaries. Designed as the board is, she is confined to its columns and rows. She is the most powerful person, but only on that board. However, the Queen's present-day counterpart has managed to free herself from earthly constraints. The first woman in space, Soviet cosmonaut Valentina Tereshkova, flew in 1963. She was followed in later years by 64 other women who broke out of Earth's orbit. The 2013 US Astronaut Class graduated equal parts, men and women. The first woman's expedition to the Moon is planned for 2024, as part of the Artemis program, whose mission it is to "land the first woman and the next man on the moon."

But the Chess Queen is firmly rooted in 21st Century culture, and she's available in a varied assortment of options. Chess Queen tattoos are displayed at the click of Chess Queen Tattoos in your browser. Plain or fancy, solo or with her king, and always crowned, she may be permanently displayed on the bodily appendage of your choice.

Earthbound and now liberated from clay, the Chess Queen piece cleans up nicely, often elegantly as befits her stature. Today, a short trip on line will find that her piece might be attired in classic flowing robes or Roman garb. Or the wannabe lady might even wear a t shirt or at least be celebrated on one at Chess Queen t shirt. Etsy offers a variety of Black Chess Queen shirts. There are also the twin offerings: her Queen and his matching king shirts, here, at least his superior height is not mandated. King and Queen share equal body size. Instant coronation is available in the Chess Queen costumes; the throne may be sold separately.

The Chess Queen has even more other ways to express herself today. For dog loving chess players, there is a canine set available complete with opposing bitches and doghouses. Cat vs Dog sets infuse stereotypes to add another level to the game's intent. In jewelry, she can be hung as pendants from ears, and necks and wrists. For couples, affordable stainless steel ring sets are inscribed with firm declarations of love. His engraving says "Her King" and hers "His Queen" and that says it all.

The Chess Queen's power on the chessboard is firmly in place. Present day Chess Queens rule.as women's power emerges from its Middle Game.

# THE QUEEN BECOMES THE
# MOST POWERFUL PIECE!

# 2

# THE IMMORTAL PROMISE IN THE IMMORTAL GAME

Is there some profound truth in the seemingly immortal game of chess that speaks to us across time? Before it appeared in 6th Century India, did the game "exist" as that fundamental part of the human condition defining our roles and our limits? David Shenk, describes the phenomena, the "History of Chess, or how 32 carved pieces on a board illuminated our understanding of war, art, science, and the human brain."[1] Is chess actually a timeless concept?

So, like mathematics, was Chess created or was it discovered? Was it present, hidden someplace in Plato's perfect forms, or did the omnipresence of warfare mandate its birth? The origin legends of Chess are profuse and maybe one of them represents the facts, but the first chess set in India, the

---

[1] Shenk, David. *The Immortal Game.* New York: Doubleday Broadway Publishing Group, 2006.

game chaturanga, used the four elements of the Indian army : chariots, elephants, infantry and cavalry. Added to the army core were the king and his general. Chess provided these little pieces the opportunity to demonstrate and develop strategic warfare while never having to leave home.

The ancient passage of chess to Persia in a tale told by Ferdowsi in the 11th Century *Shahnameh*, Greater Persia's national epic. Based on English Translations in the British Museum, the story relates the arrival in Persia of an Indian Ambassador. He offers the Persian King a board with strange pieces carved of ebony and ivory and challenges the Persian Wise Men to solve the mysteries of the game. If they fail, demonstrating their lack of intellect, they must pay tribute to the Indian King.

After a fretful night examining the possibilities of the board with its bi-colored pieces, one of them, Bozorgmehr, uncovers and declares the game's secret, and is richly rewarded by the Persian king. One assumes the Indians gnashed their teeth in despair, unaware that it was unlikely Bozorgmehr had played fair, but uncovered the game's mystery by simply bribing the Indian envoy.

Its original line-up in Persia, contained the Ruhk (chariot), Faras (horse), Al-fil (elephant), Firzan (minister), Baidaq (foot soldier) and Shah,( king). To this day, those names remain there. The king, Shah, gave the immortal game its immortal name, thanks to mispronunciation on the part of later British merchants when shah became chess. Moreover, when stymied, the opposing king became Shah mat (Persian for the "king is helpless), check mate.

8th Century Arab Muslims invaded Persia, learned chess and took it with them when they conquered Spain in 711. Unfortunately, the queen did not make the cut. She arrived in drag. Actually, even today, she remains MIA in Islamic chess where the old vizier/Firzan still stands beside the Shah. Currently, the Taliban even forbids chess along with education for women.

So quiet, so reserved, so restricted to one space that was diagonal and of the same color, the future queen, still only an advisor, was the weakest chess piece of all. The king, though likewise confined could at least access any adjacent square. Her mission was solely to protect the king; she was an ancient Secret Service man, wary, prepared to pounce. But then, without warning, that all began to fall apart, and in a very unlikely place, a 10th Century Swiss Monastery.

In a manuscript, *The Einsiedeln Poem*, preserved for over a thousand years, an anonymous Benedictine Monk, took time from his prayers to set down the modern features of the game of chess in poetry. It would be a contest of intellect; there would be no dice involved; no high-rollers need apply, The poem proceeds. The thirty-two chess pieces must be only red or white and would be named thus: rex (king), regina (queen), comes (today's bishop), eques (knight), rochus (rook), pedes (pawn). Though, finally recognized, and the only female on the board, the queen's moves are still restricted, unchanged, but finally, after 500 years, she is out of the closet.

The monk's rules actually would allow for another woman to enter the fray. An intrepid pedes who crosses the entire board to the eighth row can assume the role of the regina. But that is only if the original has been captured and has exited the board, since Christianity allowed only one wife at a time to the king. The Persian game had no such problem, since the king could have any number of firzan.

It is speculated that it was the powerful German Queen, Adelaide, wife of King Otto I and later Empress of the Holy Roman Empire, who recast the monk's vision of a woman's place from vizier to queen, wife of the king. Powerful queens had emerged in the late 10th Century, but any royal medieval queen was in a precarious position, living on the edge of disaster. Though the king was often guided by her advice. she could easily be discarded, imprisoned or banished to a nunnery. A clever, wily queen might control the king. She would also produce his heirs; the Arabic furzan had no such gift. Clearly, it seems it was a given to the Einsiedeln Monk, that the closest place to a king's had to be a Queen's.

The new found lady's simple role remained; her sole task was to protect the king and being so conscripted in movement, she stayed in her place as the weakest piece on the board. Her devotion was practical. Survival of the king was crucial, if he succumbed to an enemy, they all were ruined.

Not a pandemic virus, but a highly contagious idea, the game of chess spread all over medieval Europe. From its original incursion into Spain, it spread to Southern Germany in 1050 and Central Italy by 1061. By the 12th Century it was even incorporated into the culture of medieval chivalry, included as one of the seven essential skills of the knighthood.

Beginning in the 13th Century powerful women queens served as living models for the Chess Queen: Eleanor of Aquitaine, beautiful and bold, was the epitome of royal panache. Her brilliant court featured troubadours and storytellers and games galore, prominently the game of chess. She and her young husband, King Louis VII heeded the call for the Second Crusade and embarked on a perilous journey, amply supplied with life's necessities prominently including the mandatory chess games.

Board games had been established throughout courtly life by the 15th Century, and Isabella of Spain and her husband, Ferdinand of Aragon were avid players. Backgammon and dice and now the introduction of playing cards, kept courtiers engaged and entertained. But it was chess that was Isabella's passion. She, never lacking for verve, emerged as the queen who would not be confined to a supportive role, and initiated some dubious practices along with her prescient support of Christopher Columbus.

But the notion of the Chess Queen as bound by rules that stymied her movement had reached its plausibility, and it spilled into reality as a 64 stanza love poem, *Scachs d'amor* conceived as a chess game. Real Queens got out and about, and though still fettered to the king, their visions grew wide. The world of chess reeled as the new nervy queen, freed now, swept across the board with almost no constraint. The new Queen's Chess or the disparaged "Mad Queen's Chess" had arrived and changed the game forever. A woman, granted her freedom, was now the most powerful piece on the chess board!

Marilyn Yalom points out the game's unique space in all of then current society. "Chess you might say, had matured. It was suitable not only for lovers in the early throes of attraction, but also for spouses settled into conjugal happiness. By the late 15th Century, when the Chess Queen's supreme powers were officially codified, the game itself was at the height of its popularity, with a special meaning for couples. They could look to chess as a special space for the interchange of intellect, feeling and sexual desire. Both before and after marriage, chess offered a playing field where men and women could confront each other as equals." [2]

The Queen's mobility had turbo charged the game. Leisurely hours, games interrupted by more games of court intrigue or romance evaporated into a medieval mist and were replaced by keen edged competition. David Shenk describes the transition, "Seasoned players realized all too well ...it was an entirely new game. It was much faster and aggressive...and it was vastly more complex because at any given time, each player had many more move choices —and had to anticipate more responses from the opponent." [3]

She had help, surprisingly, in the arrival of the revolutionary printing press. Books written to explain or celebrate chess, were now more widely available in contrast to the labor-intensive manuscripts. More people could play and more did...men. The game was faster now, no longer able to sustain a leisurely day's diversion.

So as her opportunity became her undoing. and waiting men pounced, not always without misogynous intent, the game became less social and simply competitive. For the following centuries chess went public, in male only Chess Clubs and Coffee Houses.

It wasn't until the 20th Century that women effectively burst their confined space. Though she had endured centuries of mistreatment, women imitating the latent power of the Chess Queen, disturbed the false equilibrium, and got back into the game.

And so, she begins to regain power as the "New Woman" and she arrives on the scene, rolling in on wheels. The Queen of Suffrage, Susan B. Anthony, observed the scene, and felt that the bicycle had done more to liberate women than anything else in the world. Like the Chess Queen, the New

---

[2] Yalom, Marilyn, *Birth of the Chess Queen* ( New York: Harper Collins Publishers, 2004)

[3] Shenk, David, *The Immortal Game, A History of Chess* (New York: Doubleday, 2006)

Woman was free now to move across the landscape, wearing pants, bloomers actually, since confining dress codes like limiting chess rules were simply made to be broken.

Yet, some might cite the typewriter as the major agent of liberation. Mostly employed by women, this revolutionary mechanical device set them free to earn their own salaries. By 1900 according to the census 94.9% of typists were unmarried women.

Across the board and across the political and social scene, the landscape rumbled with feminine agitation. Then World War I arrived and women replaced men in the military. Not in active combat, like the Queen on the chess board, but by replacing them at home. They were freed to do administrative battle at home, while the men were released to fight abroad.

The rest is history.

## QUEENS : BLACK = WHITE

# 3

# THE BLACK QUEEN'S RISE

The first Black Queen, the Queen of Sheba, was a most remarkable woman. Stories abound and derive from a variety of sources, Jewish, Islamic and Arabian, all tell her tale, sometimes in conflict. She was a woman of great intrigue and interest, providing tempting fodder for tall tales. We piece together what is possibly factual, and enjoy the parts that are probable. Though in the 10th Century BC she would be an aspirational prototype of the chess board's Black Queen, she could later serve as a remarkable role model for the newly mobile 15th Century chess piece. It is estimated that her trip across Africa to Jerusalem, took years, and can serve as a forecaster of the Persian Vizier's long journey to 15th Century transgendered freedom.

Stories abound proclaiming her beauty and brains. The Bible Kings 1 has the queen, upon hearing of Judea's King Solomon's wisdom she travelled to Jerusalem to test him with difficult questions. As befits a woman of her stature, she packed well, including gifts for her host: about 5 tons of gold, exotic spices such as turmeric and ginger, precious stones and rare wood.

The Bible says " King Solomon gave the Queen of Sheba everything she asked for." 2 Chronicles 9: 1-12 which might have included a son with a faultless line of descent: grandfather, King David, grandmother Bathsheba. The story contends that she was tricked into his bed, though the Bible narrative has her gob smacked by his wealth and possessions and probably enamored by his charm. "How fortunate are your wives," (all 200 of them.). He might even have made her an honest woman. #201.

Pregnant and now a convert to Solomon's Judaism, The Queen of Sheba returned home, and gave birth to their son, Menelik. When he ascended to the throne, a royal dynasty commenced which would rule Ethiopia with few interruptions for close to three thousand years. His lineage would persist until 1974., when 225 generations later the famed Emperor Haile Selassie would be forced to abdicate the throne.

The Islamic tradition claims Bilquis as the Queen of Sheba. She appears in the Quran and injects a bit of fancy into her meeting with King Solomon. Prior to her arrival at the King's court, Solomon had been advised by his jinn, a genie, that Bilquis had hairy legs and the hooves of a goat. Though acclaimed the wisest of all, Solomon was easily persuaded, and he ordered a glass floor built in front of his throne. The plan worked. Bilquis mistaking the glass for water, raised her skirts and in fact did reveal one leg, densely covered with thick black hair. One might mistakenly believe that a depilatory is a modern invention. Not so. Solomon ordered the jinn to produce such a cream as the modern cosmetic. Though the text does not comment on its efficacy, with or without hair, it didn't prevent him, Solomon, from either marrying her himself, or passing her off to a friend.

Other traditions celebrate this first Black Queen, called Makeda to Ethiopians, and Bilikisu to the Nigerian Lgebu people, who claim her burial site. She was a Black Queen, of very dark skin, testified to in the song of Solomon, 1:4. the object of his love, declaring, "I am Black and beautiful." She was as Black as the Chess Queen, and clearly as intrepid.

Centuries later, history records two more Black Queens. The first appears in 14th Century England. She was the unfaithful Queen Isabella, described as the She Wolf of France. Brilliant and beautiful, she was a formidable player in the power game, an early model of the powerful Chess Queen, yet still a pawn in the hands of kings.

As was the custom, Isabella's father, King Phillip of France, arranged a political marriage for all four of his children. Isabella was betrothed to King Edward II of England. At the time of her marriage in 1308 the twelve- year-old bride to-be packed a hoard of dresses and jewelry, two gold crowns, gold and silver dinnerware and 419 yards of linen. Isabella's optics were devastating, Geoffrey of Paris describes the bride as "the beauty of beauties…in the kingdom if not in all Europe."

Surrounded by the drama of the moment, and the political consequences of their union, in 1308 the French city of Boulogne-sur-mer was surrounded by the luxurious tents of the assembled royalty of Europe, including seven kings and queens. The assembled royalty gathered like so many chess pieces vying for control of the European chess board.

Unfortunately for the child bride, her 23-year-old husband preferred his close male companion, a soldier, Piers Gaveston whose miserable personality alienated him from all but endeared him to Edward. In England now, Edward immediately sidelined the young Queen, choosing Gaveston to sit next to him at their English wedding celebration, possibly presaging the 21 Century same sex marriages.

Ultimately estranged from King Edward II, whose homosexual relationships persisted, despite fathering four offspring, Isabella returned to France in 1325. Edward had become increasingly unwilling to protect his wife, and their relationship was antagonistic, warlike. Isabella with the help of her lover, Roger Mortimer, planned to retaliate by raising an army to invade England. But she needed the wherewithal to take back the ascendancy of the English throne.

Isabella would reiterate her own experience, and would betroth her own son, the future Edward III to Phillipa Hainaut. With the dowry obtained by this arrangement, Isabella and Mortimer would raise the army which would ultimately invade England, and successfully depose the king.

The future Queen Phillipa, the first Black Queen, was of Black Moorish ancestry. Described by Bishop Stapledon "The lady whom we saw has not uncomely hair, between blue-Black and brown…Moreover she is all brown of skin all over, much like her father. And she will be of age nine years on St. John's Day, next to come, her mother says."

Phillipa was clearly a good choice, able to thread the needle between the growing antagonism between her domineering mother-in-law and her husband, equally determined Edward III. Isabella's reign as Queen Dowager was finally terminated when her son arranged a coup and ousted his mother and her consort, Mortimer. Isabella was banished to her own Castle Rising in Norfolk. Mortimer was simply executed.

Queen now, Phillipa and Edward enjoyed an amicable marriage, though sadly, of her fourteen children she outlived nine. Three of her children died of the Black Plague in 1348. Her oldest though, became the famed Edward, the Black prince, a Black King to stand alongside his mother, the Black Queen.

Edward II was kinder to Isabella, allowing her to live surrounded by luxury in her castle. Her lifestyle was opulent, including minstrels, huntsmen and grooms and other amenities. She was permitted her travel around England and took part in negotiations with France. Then at the end, this tired woman eschewed it all. Donning the dull habit, she joined the Poor Clares, a contemplative order of Catholic nuns. A Chess Queen defrocked.

England's 2nd Black Queen Charlotte, Sophia Charlotte of Mecklenburg-Strelitz, was enormously qualified, her ethnic designation is questioned, though not in the current Netflix series, *Bridgerton*, where the queen as portrayed by Golda Rosheuvel emerges as clearly biracial. The historic underpinnings for this portrayal emanate from historian Mario de Valdes y

Concom who claims that the Queen, though German, was directly descended from the Black branch of the Portuguese Royal Family.

Charlotte became queen of Britain and Ireland when she married King George III in September 1761. According to the Royal Family's official website, the couple exchanged their vows six hours after the 17-year-old arrived in England and they met for the first time. On that happy day, no seer emerged to foretell the sadness ahead and their union though hasty, would be mutually loving and prolific; Queen Charlotte bore 15 children, 13 of whom survived to adulthood.

Bright and competent, an accomplished harpsichordist, Charlotte invested herself in music, a passion she would share with her husband, King George, founder of the Royal Academy of the Arts. The Royal Collection trust affirms that a little 8-year-old boy performed for the Royals, playing the organ as Charlotte sang. He was an amazing prodigy, Wolfgang Amadeus Mozart, who was on loan to the Queen's court.

But the party ended when after 25 years of marital accord, George morphed into "Mad King George" succumbing to a series of debilitating incidences as portrayed by Nigel Hawthorne in the film, *The Madness of King George*. In 1788, the King experienced a month-long manic episode, the first of four ensuing events which destroyed their formerly loving relationship.

English history has not been particularly supportive of Queen Charlotte, Charles Dickens refers to her in the opening lines of *A Tale of Two Cities*. *"There was a king with a large jaw and a queen with a plain face on the throne of England."* The one statue of Charlotte, in a small square in Bloomsbury, was until a century later, incorrectly assumed to be Queen Anne.

Episodes of *Bridgerton* somewhat repair her image, and across the pond, one southern city celebrates the overlooked Queen. Charlotte, North Carolina, the "Queen City" was settled by a wave of Scotch-Irish Presbyterians in about 1755. The proud founders inadvertently honored the future Revolutionary War, antagonist.

Queen Charlotte, the second Black Queen, built Windsor's Frogmore House in 1801 as a country retreat for her unmarried daughters. Three centuries later ironically, Megan Markle, the bi-racial Duchess of Sussex, moved into the newly refurbished home and nursery prior to the birth of her son, Archie Mountbatten-Windsor. When they chose to separate from the royal family, the prospect, though remote, of another Black Queen was history.

Meghan and Harry remained through January 2020, when she and Harry severed their royal ties and departed England. In a widely acclaimed interview with Oprah Winfrey, the fault lines in her relationship with "The Firm," as the royal family is called, became clear. Meghan revealed the fact that she had been "silenced." There was no room available for an outspoken feminist's opinions. The culture clash was inevitable ; no pawns need apply.

## *PAWN TRANS*

# 4

## PAWN TO QUEEN

Miracles happen in the game of chess. In Persian games, elephants glide like pigeons in a diagonal line across the board. Castles are equally mobile and humble pawns upon reaching the back rank, become Firzan, (viziers). On western chessboards, the same lowly foot soldiers who persist, ascribe to the most powerful of all pieces, the indomitable Chess Queen.

Again, chess demonstrated one of its innate reasons for being, since a "cat can look at a queen, " the universal truth that somehow, somewhere, the lowest classes may overcome. The young woman who saved the cinders was fortunately only one shoe away from living happily ever after as the Prince's bride, the future queen.

Benjamin Franklin, an avid player, declared that, "Life is a game of chess, in which we have often points to gain, and competitors and adversaries to contend with."[4] The pushy pawn, struggling across the board, is routinely attacked by rooks and bishops and yes, even other pawns. Now, nearing the enemy's first row, the opposing pieces conspire to prevent the creation of yet another powerful woman.

Lewis Carroll's Alice in *Through the Looking Glass* is terribly confused when confronted with two queens, one red, one white, who have simply fallen asleep, leaning on her. "I don't think it ever happened before, that anyone had to take care of two queens asleep at once! No, not in all The History of England—it couldn't you know, because there never was more than one Queen at a time."

---

[4] See p299 Schenk

Clearly, Alice's queenship is a farce as her celebratory banquet descends into mayhem, the White Queen "instead of the Queen, a leg of mutton is sitting in her chair…and the Red Queen…had suddenly dwindled down to the size of a little doll and now on the table, merrily running around after her own shawl….[5]

Spoiler alert. Lewis Carroll constructed the plot of Through the Looking Glass as a chess game, laying out the moves in a deliberate plan for Alice's ascent to royalty, his plan, *"White Pawn (Alice) to play and win in eleven moves"*

Folk music was a natural place for "Pawns" to ascend since it spoke to the everyday lives of working-class Americans and drew its inspiration from its immigrant roots. Country folk music spoke to the soul of working class Americans and to the blue-collar American way of life.

It had been inspired by the American folk music tradition which had its roots in Celtic music, early music of the British Isles, singing cowboys, French folk music, and African-American music. traditions The term "folklore", which was coined in 1846 by the English antiquarian William Thoms who disdainfully described the traditions, customs, and superstitions of the uncultured classes.

From these rich sources, talented "Queens" arose, travelling across the rank and file of challenges and opportunities. The time was right for the first, Kitty Wells, who paved the way for women in country music. When Ellen Muriel Deason became Kitty Wells, in the 1950's women's voices were not generally heard. Women could not headline a concert, and there existed an unspoken prohibition against playing two women's records back-to-back. Not really a problem, since very few songs were written for women at that time.

But then county music got real with the lingering disruption from World War II. Then men began to sing about drinking and cheating and Kitty found her place. With a decided twang, in a voice that could penetrate to the back walls she belted out the numbers that would make her the Queen of Country Music.

Her defining moment came when the male ego was attacked in Hank Thompson's "The Wild Side of Life" There the singer expresses regret that his bride-to-be has left him for another man whom she had met in a roadhouse. The spurned lover sings that "God didn't make Honky Tonk Angels" Kitty answered back, big time with "It Wasn't God who Made Honky Tonk Angels."

---

[5] Carroll, Lewis, *Through the Looking Glass* (New York, 1885)

[Verse 1].
As I sit here tonight the jukebox playing
The tune about the wild side of life
As I listen to the words you are saying
It brings memories when I was a trusting wife
[Verse 2]
It's a shame that all the blame is on us women
It's not true that only you men feel the same
From the start most every heart that's ever broken
Was because there always was a man to blame

It wasn't God who made honky tonk angels
As you said in the words of your song
Too many times married men think they're still single
And that's caused many a good girl to go wrong

As the chess pawn nears becoming crowned a queen, her opponents attack, fearful of her impending strength. Kitty Wells' feminist statement was a rather daring one to make in 1952, particularly in the conservative, male-dominated realm of country music. Adultery from the point of view of the cheated-upon woman was so contrary to the chauvinist mind as to be unspeakable Though some manner of convoluted reasoning, the NBC radio network found the lyric "suggestive," and like the Grand Ole Opry banned its performance by Wells.

But "It Wasn't God..." struck a note and resounded big time with her audience, and Kitty Wells' first recording single sold more than 800,000 copies making her the first solo female country artist to have a number 1 record on the charts and turned Kitty into a Country Star. Attitudes towards women in country music were swiftly changing and Kitty Wells continued to enjoy the success and acclaim that her talents deserved. In 1991 she was awarded the Grammy Lifetime Achievement award and with her success and influence on women in country music, she earned the title, Queen of Country Music."

Like the Queen Duo in Alice's adventures, Fabulous Dolly Parton has risen to the rank, though she is anxious to disavow the accolade. The second acclaimed Queen of Country Music wants to share the glory with other very talented women. Speaking with *Nightline* in a new tell-all interview, Dolly gives the details on this great offense, explaining why it bothers her so much and how she doesn't feel it fits. Reporter David Wright said that often people view her as "The Queen of Country Music" because of her massive success and lengthy career.

"Well, I'm not the queen though," she said with a smile. "The queen of country music is Kitty Wells. And then there are the others like Loretta and Tammy. " I'll take whatever title they want to give me," Dolly added. "Sometimes they call me the queen of country music and I take offense to that because that's not fair to the ones that had that title before. I don't know what I am…but I'm still at it – I'm still grateful I'm still here."

From a humble start, fourth child in a family of twelve, growing up poor in a farming family in Locust Ridge, Tennessee, she rose to become the most honored female country performer of all time. In a conversation with Oprah Winfrey, she commented that without a family, she and Carl Dean, her husband of 54 years, have no children, she declared she'd been completely free to work. And so, she did, starting young as a radio performer and recording singles at the age of 13 and not stopping, looking beautiful and still in voice while past 70.

In the course of her fabulous career Dolly Parton has won an incredible number of awards, including 8 Grammy Awards and 10 Country Music Association Awards. Two other aspects of her accomplishments are a large part of her contributions. One is commercial, her dream resort, Dollywood, is inspired by Dolly Parton's warm childhood memories growing up in the Great Smoky Mountains. The Website further explains that Dollywood's DreamMore Resort is your Smoky Mountain home away from home filled with family experiences worth sharing together.

Childless Dolly Parton, in her interview with Oprah, explained that "I didn't have children because I believed that God didn't want me to have kids so everybody's kids could be mine." So, she began the Imagination Library to benefit the children in her home county in East Tennessee to foster the love of reading to help them realize their dreams. Dolly Parton's Imagination Library is a book gifting program the gives free books to children from birth to age five, in participating communities within the United State, United Kingdom, Canada, Australia and the Republic of Ireland. Last tally had the total number of gift books at 152,366,795.

Dolly the Pawn become Queen was unique in that she never forgot the rank where she began and the other little pawns in place beside her.

Eva Peron (Evita) was not the only impoverished woman to pass from pawn to queen, but she was certainly the most beloved. Eva arrived at the height of power atop the country of Argentina by way of her man, the president Juan Peron. Her story was long, though her life was short.

In rural Argentina, in 1919, it was not unusual for a wealthy man, or maybe even a poor man, to have multiple families. And so, it was with her father, Juan Duarte, who just before abandoning his children to poverty and disgrace, cranked out a document declaring his paternity, thus sharing his surname.

Eva Duarte, age 15, escaped Junin, her province and travelled to Buenos Aires where she quickly relieved herself of her companion musician boyfriend and her black hair. Blonde Eva ramped up her acting and then her business acumen, and by 1943 she was one of the highest paid radio actresses in the country. No matter their 24-year age difference, love struck when Eva met Juan at a gala to honor earthquake victims. The ground shook and the woman who was his mistress for the following year, became his wife when Juan Peron married Eva Duarte in 1945.

Then he became president of Argentina and Eva became the most popular idol of her times. Though she enjoyed the trappings of power, with her first-hand experience of poverty and discrimination, she immediately engaged herself in the current battles for social justice. Among her other causes were two in particular: her self-founded Eva Peron Foundation, and the first large-scale female political party, the Female Peronist Party advocates for women's suffrage, long delayed and finally passed in 1947.

But it was her work and success with the Eva Peron Foundation that elevated her to popular devotion. Scenes of her meeting the poor who appealed for help to the Foundation, openly kissing and embracing the sick and wounded elevated her to Catholic Argentina's vision of sainthood. Despite declining health, Eva continued to work endlessly at her task, energized by the very presence of the evil of poverty as she saw it. Her 20-hour days were a fevered attempt to beat the cancer growing within her, to eradicate as much injustice as possible before the end.

Eva Peron died of cervical cancer at the age of 33. The country was devastated, deeply mourning their idol. But events ensued; politics roiled. Juan Peron was ousted in a coup in 1955, and Eva's embalmed corpse disappeared. The military dictatorship now in charge issued a ban on Peronism, and for 16 years, the corpse was secretly buried in a crypt in Milan, Italy.

Juan Peron emerged from his exile in Spain and was again elected president of Argentina in 1973. At his death in 1974, Eva's body was returned to be displayed alongside him then safely ensconced in a most secure tomb. A marble floor contains a trapdoor leading to a compartment with two coffins, below which is yet another compartment, accessible only by another trapdoor. Therein lies the final resting place of the fabulous Evita.

Eva Duarte Peron remains vibrant in Andrew Lloyd Weber's popular musical, *Evita* and in film, where Madonna channels her, singing, "Don't cry for me Argentina, the truth is I never left you." Argentina still returns her love in memory.

The journey across the board, from pawn to queen is hazardous. Circumstances intrude and sometimes destroy but the power when finally acquired is priceless.

*ATTACK!*

# 5

# KING SQUARE CONTENDERS

The Chess Queen, became the victim of her own success. She was a liberated lady chess piece now, free to move anywhere she might, more powerful than every other piece, an Amazon in a board full of men. Maybe the king should start protecting her.

But factors had combined and quashed the game for women. The lovely long and romantic chess match had been the court's pleasant pastime, became jet charged. The queen and also the bishop had been freed. He could travel across the board in a deadly diagonal now but anything he could do; she could do better. The new "Mad Queen" reigned over the board, but the real Queens' kingdoms had been mostly replaced by nation states, and the royal women stayed home.

Chess's origins in military conflict had favored men and as the game lost its social use, and professional chess players emerged, the friendly often romantic male-female matches became obsolete and women were essentially barred from competition. Respectable women would never engage in such a public display and again chess mirrored reality. The Renaissance woman, like the Chess Queen, would function largely at the behest of her male handlers and as political entities evolved in to the nation-state, noble women were politely excused from relevance. The role of the woman was largely redefined. Women who might engage in unladylike practices such as riding horses, were to observe decorum by only riding side saddle. Only the Chess Queen piece could exercise her strength in the male's world of prejudice and power.

One queen acted as an exception, Maria Theresa, the queen of the extensive Hapsburg Dominion, asserted that, had she not been almost always pregnant, she would have gone into battle herself.[6] While a queen who was reigning effectively to protect her kingdom, she gave birth to 16 heirs, twelve of them daughters, all first-named Maria, after herself.

Though her progeny were married off to strengthen royal alliances, it was her youngest daughter, Maria Antonia, who was most notorious. Married to the French Dauphine during the French Revolution, now Queen Marie Antoinette, famously suggested that the starving people who had no bread to eat could solve their problem. " Let them eat cake," she suggested. Though ignorant of the sad lives of her pawns, this queen was only trying to be practical. She ended poorly, her pawns, her little people put an end to her, and checked her king.

Some centuries later in 1872 a "pawn" aspired to be not a queen, but the United States President. The universal intent of the chess game continued to reflect reality when Vitoria Claflin Woodhull was nominated by the Equal Rights Party as their presidential candidate. This upstart contender who supported women's suffrage and equal rights had every reason to crusade for women.

Stories abound of Victoria Woodhull, from her earliest moments as the seventh of ten children born to Roxanna Hummel and Rueben "Old Buck" Claflin in the town of Homer, Licking County, Ohio in 1838 to her career as an outspoken advocate for women's rights. Given the beatings and maltreatment on the part of her father, it wasn't surprising that at age 15, she married a self-proclaimed "doctor" Canning Woodhull. What he hadn't proclaimed was his womanizing and alcoholism. These habits ended the marriage after the birth of their two children, Byron, his intellectual handicap credited to his father's drinking, and Zulu, later name Zula.

Like the queen's freedom to move across the chessboard, Victoria gathered up her young sister, Tennessee, and moved to New York City. Somehow, they gained the favor of Cornelius Vanderbilt, who went on to consider marriage to Tennessee, a prospect discouraged by the Vanderbilt family. He did, however, bankroll a Wall Street Brokerage for the sisters and later using their new found wealth, they founded their own newspaper, *Woodhull and Claflin's Weekly*.

Though barely stirring, the winds of women's liberation were forming, and Victoria Woodhull would not be contained. Her ideas were startling and upsetting in this proper Victorian era. Given the injustices of her first marriage, and reacting to the stigma attached to divorced women, she made clear her conviction that a woman had every right to dissolve an unbearable

---

[6] Holborn, Hajo (1982) A History of Modern Germany: 1648-1840 Princeton: Princeton University Press

marriage. Furthermore, she declared more untenable notions in a speech at New York's Steinway Hall on November 20, 1871.

Yes, I am a free lover. I have an unalienable , constitutional and natural right to love as long or as short a period as I can; to change that love every day if I please, and with that right neither you or any law you can frame have any right to interfere.[7]

Victoria went on breaking tradition, marrying twice and divorcing once. Her undoing came when she exposed the infidelity of the revered preacher, Henry Ward Beecher. But she was still nominated for United States President by the Equal Rights Party, and her nomination was confirmed at the convention on June 6, 1872. At the same time, they nominated the former slave and abolitionist, Frederick Douglass to serve as her Vice President.

Her presidential candidacy was doomed by the all-male voting public .and additionally by her age. She would not be the qualifying age, 35, till six months after the March Inauguration. .

Victoria Woodhull was the first of bold women who would aspire to the president's square, the former king's place on the board. The second, Belva Lockwood ran as a candidate for the National Equal Rights Party, in 1884 and again in 1888, in both cases with a male vice-president candidate. Alfred H. Love her first run's choice was unaware of his selection and wasn't ready to play the role of the country's 2nd Gentleman. Horrified he refused and was replaced with Charles Stuart Weld, a better choice, as the son of active progressives.

Belva was well acquainted with rejection. Widowed twice, a single mother armed with nothing but determination, she prevailed over discrimination against women in college, then law school and finally, in the United States Supreme Court. Belva, with an instinct for the eye of the storm, gathered her daughter, Lura, and in 1866 decamped from her home in upstate New York and moved to Washington, DC.

Had she not encountered enough prejudices in New York, she was met with a new batch when she applied for the bar in Maryland. She had to question the dubious intelligence of the judge who informed her that she should be denied admittance due to the fact that God had ordained that women would never be equal to men. Shocked though maybe not surprised, Belva's rebuttal infuriated the judge and she was removed from the courtroom.

Belva persisted and ultimately built a successful practice culminating in the drafting and passage of an anti-discrimination law which allowed this "unequal" woman and other women to practice law in federal courts, most notable the United States Supreme Court. Just one tremendous challenge remained for the determined advocate of feminism.

---

[7] Goldsmith, Barbara (1998). **Other Powers.** New York, Alfred A. Knopf.

As a harbinger of the future liberation of women, Belva Lockwood surprised herself in her second presidential run, and everyone else. She received about 4.000 votes, possibly from the women in Wyoming, in 1869 the only state to pass women's suffrage. Surely, some right minded men also supported a woman, maybe in the safety of the secret ballot.

It wasn't until 1964 that another woman Margaret Chase Smith would be nominated, though she removed herself from contention after the first ballot at the Republican National Convention. In their attempts to win the presidency, eleven women would follow in the intervening years, until the advent of Hillary Rodham Clinton in 2008 Her arrival would be eclipsed by the charismatic Barack Obama. No matter, in 2016 Hilary Clinton went on to win the election against Donald Trump. She bested him in the popular vote by over 3 million votes, only to be defeated by the Electoral College.

Circumstances might result in the Vice President's moving into the King's space, the White House. A most unusual relationship at its time could at least theoretically have moved a Black slave into that position. Had she lived, Julia Chinn, the common law wife of our ninth vice president, and mother of his two daughters might have held that honor. So unusually liberal for his times, Richard Mentor Johnson, entrusted the running of his plantation to his slave/wife, and gifted his daughters with his name, though in fact he "owned" his wife, a gift from his father. Despite the uproar caused by his lifestyle, Martin Van Buren, chose him as his running mate in 1836, four years after Julia Chinn had passed away. A victim of cholera, her burial site is unknown.

Another liberal leaning Democrat deliberately crossed the gender line when Walter Mondale chose Geraldine Ferraro as his running mate in the 1984 presidential election . The strong winds were behind her at the nominating convention, the epitome of the American Dream: a woman whose father was an immigrant, she'd made the leap from poverty to politics, eschewing her husband's name to honor her mother. Their chances looked almost good then, though they were pitted against the popularity of the current office holders, Ronald Reagan and George H.W. Bush. To ensure victory the rumor mongers pounced, and with innuendo abounding regarding her husband John Zaccaro's finances, they were doomed to failure. They lost the electoral vote in every state other than Mondale's home state, Minnesota, and in the District of Columbia. Another hope for women dashed.

Though her intelligence and competence were remarkable legacies, Geraldine Ferraro was responsible for an enduring title for women. Without her husband's name she was still "Miss Ferraro," a misnomer for a married woman. Her husband was not "Mr. Ferraro," and she never used the married title, Mrs. Zaccaro. Two years later, the New York Times changed its policy, initiating the now universal "MS" to identify an undefined marital state for women.

Maybe now the Chess Queen's moment has at long last arrived. Joseph Robinette Biden chose Kamala Harris to be his Vice President in his successful 2020 bid for election to President of the United States of America. It's entirely possible that the V.P./Queen might occupy the Commander-in Chief/King's square. Or in time, the 47th or counting might see a queen as POTUS. And it may be either the Black Queen or the White Queen who makes that move.

# THE QUEEN IS OFF THE BOARD

# 6

# THE WOMEN THAT MADE IT HAPPEN

Some women were willing to die for their rightful place in society, their right to vote, comparable to a gambit in chess, the opening which involves the deliberately planned loss of material.

Two British suffragettes behaved outlandishly; both were willing to die for women's freedom. One actually did. It wasn't Marion Wallace-Dunlop, though she stated happily that her death in prison would definitely help the cause of suffrage. Her bold graffiti post in the June, 1909 protest, had earned her a month's stay in Holloway Prison. Immediately after she was sentenced, she demanded to be treated as a political prisoner and she stated "… as a matter of principle, not only for my own sake but for the sake of others who might come after me, I am refusing all food until this matter is settled to my satisfaction."[8] She thus established herself as the first hunger striker in recorded history.

Emily Wilding Davis (1872-1913) was the suffragette who died for the cause. A bright young woman, she took classes at Oxford University though they wouldn't admit to it. No degree was available for women at that time. Her teaching job was just too tame for Emily and she quit and joined up with the raging suffrage movement.

Maybe it was in the "Wilding" part of her name that shaped her, but Emily Wilding Davidson, after prison, went on to protest and finally perform

---

[8] Spartacus Educational.com/Wallace-Dunlop.htm

a foolish yet courageous act.[9] At the Epsom Derby, on June 4, 1913, with a round-trip railroad ticket in her pocket, and holding up two suffragette flags, she ducked under the fence and on to the track, facing the raging field of oncoming horses. Anmer, King George V's entry crashed into her before she could bestow her flags on him, a ridiculously futile misadventure. She died in hospital four days later, a madwoman to the press, a heroine in suffragette eyes, the queen's freedom misapplied.

When the indomitable Elizabeth Cady Stanton and Quaker Lucretia Mott launched the women's suffrage movement in the United States, at the Seneca Falls Women's Rights Convention in 1848, women's rights were basically non-existent. If a woman worked, did laundry or cleaned houses, her salary belonged to her husband. In the case of the rare divorce, the children were likewise, automatically the man's.

Their **Declaration of Sentiments,** issued at the convention, begins by asserting the equality of all men and women and reiterates that both genders are endowed with unalienable rights to life, liberty, and the pursuit of happiness. It argues that women are oppressed by the government and the patriarchal society of which they are a part. These sentiments were strongly endorsed by an attendee and, then controversial former slave, Frederick Douglass.

By the turn of the 20th Century, only four states, Wyoming, Colorado, Utah, and Idaho, allowed women to vote. Small wonder that no female presidential aspirant had conducted a credible run until the 21st Century. For a variety of poor reasons, the cause, votes for women, languished for the years following the convention, until 1910 when suffragist Alice Paul returned from her activist days as a suffragette in Britain.

Alice Paul had a single goal. She would change the rules of the game in the same way that the game of chess had liberated the queen. She would give women a rule which freed them to participate in an effective way. Alice moved deliberately, in a well-planned, step by step procedure to cause the passage of the 19th Amendment to the United States Constitution. This breakthrough piece of legislation, sub-titled *Women's Suffrage,* would insure that "The right of citizens of the United States to vote shall not be denied or abridged by the United States or by any State on account of sex."

As ever, when the male chess pieces, and their female queen are threatened, the pieces react with venom. Alice, joined now by her co equal conspirator, the "infamous red-head," Lucy Burns, antagonized the men on March 3, 1913 when she kicked off the first and most spectacular women's march. About 5,000 women and some men joined to demonstrate for passage of the "Anthony Amendment," named for famed suffragist Susan B. Anthony.

---

[9] Ibid. Emily Wilding Davison

Deranged at the sight of women's assertion of their rights, the assembled crowd mostly male and generally drunk, was in Washington to celebrate the inauguration of anti-suffrage President-elect Woodrow Wilson. They broke loose and a melee ensued in which the men stormed the marchers, halting the women, attacking them physically and destroying their displays. Only the intervention of the cavalry, called in despair, quelled the mayhem. Like knight pieces, they rode their horses into the mobs.

Alice and Lucy would move on buoyed in their movement by the adverse publicity resultant with the March fiasco, only to be confronted by even greater male animosity.

Their use of blatant truths, displayed by pickets, the Silent Sentinels, finally undid President Wilson, whereby they were arrested on contrived charges, and sentenced to jail terms. Hunger strikes brought out more reprisals from jailers, but garnered the condemnation of the press and the embarrassment of the administration.

Like so many "foot soldiers" suffragists were inspired by the stalwart determination of Alice Paul and Lucy Burns. The most independent and iconoclastic , Inez Milholland, road astride her stallion, Grey Dawn, at the head of the March 3rd parade. Hair flying, cape flowing the "Most Beautiful Suffragist.," again used the knight's ploy, and rode her steed directly into the wild bands of men blocking the parade.

Inez was equally devoted to the cause and to her own independence. Current custom was never a concern and when Eugene Jan Boissevain, a Dutchman, agreed to her marriage proposal, the woman's vote, though not yet granted, was still not allowed to her since she was no longer a citizen. Sure that she'd overcome, at this point not feeling good, Inez took on a recruiting train trip. She joined women who would take their stories elsewhere. They would move in dedicated train cars, in straight lines on railroad tracks across the checkerboard of America's states.

Mid speech, in October, 1916, on a stage in Los Angeles, Inez collapsed, and sadly, despite every effort to save her with repeated blood transfusions, she died the following November, a young, vibrant leader, age 31.

Like Inez, more and more women rose from the ranks, determined to change that which denied them first class citizenship. At age 73, suffragist Mary Nolan's age and infirmity did now preclude her from abuse during the infamous "Night of Terror" in her sentencing to the Occoquan Workhouse. She begged, "I'll come with you, don't drag me. I have a lame foot. But I was jerked down the stairs and into the dark."[10]

Rose Winslow's abuse was also physical. She arrived from Poland to America as an infant because her parents wanted her to become a citizen of

---

[10]Stevens, Doris, *Jailed for Freedom,* Edited by Carol O'Hare(1995) Troutdale, Oregon: New Sage Press. p.123

a "free country." At age eleven she was put to work in a fourteen-hour shift weaving hosiery in a Pennsylvania Mill. This experience gave her tuberculosis and a firm resolve to aid women workers by allowing them to vote. While confined to the hospital ward, along with Alice Paul, she entered onto a hunger strike, publicly calling out the administration's refusal to grant suffrage.

Maud Younger was not force fed; she fed others. She was dubbed "The Millionaire Waitress" since she was both. In a role reversal, the queen aspired to be pawn After a stint in a New York City settlement house, the San Francisco socialite took a job as a waitress, recognizing the urgency of the vote for working women

Harriot *Stanton* Blatch was as her name implies, the daughter of famed suffragist, Elizabeth Cady Stanton. Zealous to carry out her mother's mission, she worked tirelessly to revitalize the post-convention sagging suffragists.

Some famous women were suffragist supporters, some were celebrity foot soldiers. Among them were Helen Keller, Jeanette Rankin, Dorothy Day, and Katherine Hepburn. Many more, unsung heroines contributed their time and talents, picketing and protesting, facing hostile crowds and prison. Brave women served, such as Mable Vernon, Vida Milholland, Inez' sister, and mother and daughter, Lucy Branham who shared a name and a passion.

Black women formed their own groups, and in 1896, they founded the National Association of Colored Women. They could build on their history of exceptional women who boldly confronted the entrenched walls of the small-minded traditions of their times.

Literally standing tall in words and stature, over six-foot, Sojourner Truth (1797-1883) was the most eloquent of the earliest Black Suffragists. As a New Yorker, having been sold first at age nine for $100. and a flock of sheep, she was finally freed when the New York Anti-Slavery law was passed in 1827. So ahead of her times, so brave, she changed her given name to become Sojourner Truth and commenced her lifelong mission to gain equality for all women black and white.

Along the way, her journey took her to Akron, Ohio where she delivered her most famous speech, "Ain't I a Woman? Where she pointed out the contrast between the social acceptance of white women as opposed to black women. In yet another speech, she was interrupted and accused of being a man. Flaunting all convention, Sojourner tore open her shirt to display her breasts; no doubt she was a woman.

Ever prescient, she anticipated the eventuality of the Abolitionist movement, where black men would be granted the vote, and black women would be denied, having had words with the respected Frederick Douglass. Sojourner commented on the issue in 1867, when female suffrage was still very much being debated: "I feel that I have the right to have just as much as a man. There is a great stir about colored men getting their rights, but not a word about the colored women; and if colored men get their rights, and colored women not theirs, the colored men will be masters over the women, and it will be just as bad as it was before."

Ida B. Wells-Barnett, (1862-1931) had even more on her mind than votes for women. In 1884, she was peacefully riding in a train car reserved for white women, when three burly train workers approached and dragged her from the car. She'd paid her money for a ticket and was furious at her treatment, so she sued and won. A small victory, though, since the verdict was overthrown by the Tennessee Supreme Court. One wonders if she got her ticket money back.

But Ida was not discouraged. She was a journalist as well as an educator. One of her dear friends was lynched and her newspaper, the *Memphis Free Speech*, published extensive information on the injustice of white mob violence. So the white mob turned on her instead, burned down her press and drove her from Memphis. She escaped to Chicago and championed her causes, especially the crime of black lynching. Ever bold in the face of discrimination, she famously marched in the white section of Alice Paul's March, 1913 parade.

Mary Church Terrell (1863-1954) majored in Classics at Oberlin College, where she edited *The Oberlin Review*, and became one of the first African-American women to attend the institution, returning again to earn her master's degree in 1888. After receiving her degrees, she embarked upon a distinguished career as an activist and journalist. Along with Ida B. Wells-Barnett becoming one of the founding members of the National Association for the Advancement of Colored People (NAACP).

Although Mary Church Terrell was a member of the National American Woman Suffrage Association, it was to Alice Paul's Congressional Union she turned to join the suffragist's picket line demonstrating at the White House.

Chess pieces support and defend their same color cohorts on the board, The male players, the rooks and bishops and knights and even the lowly pawns will position themselves to defend their Queen. Many fair-minded men also supported votes for women. Dudley Field Malone and his fellow lawyer, Matthew O'Brien worked feverously to free the Silent Sentinels from prison. Theodore Roosevelt encouraged Republicans to vote for the Anthony Amendment. New Yorker Colonel William Boyce Thompson put his money into the mix. He contributed ten thousand dollars to the suffrage campaign, "one hundred dollars for each of the pickets who went to prison because she stood at the gates of the White House, asking for the passage of the suffrage measure."[11]

Despite the dedication of so many women whose sole concern was simply

---

[11] Ibid p.138

having congress create a new rule, an amendment, there were women who favored a more piecemeal method, one which was more palatable to the biased President. Carrie Chapman Catt, influential president of the National American Women's Suffrage Association actively supported Wilson's state-by-state approach, and opposed Alice Paul and Lucy Burns. She played the part of the opposing Queen.

Ironically, the Black Women Leaders were confronted with a barrage of problems, among which was the rights of all women to vote. White Suffragists, despite their rhetoric advocating equality, rarely included black women in their organizations; discrimination was largely the norm in their times. Additionally, the Suffragist leaders were so determined to win their cause, they would fear alienating their biased members and losing membership and political clout.

Black women simply formed their own groups, and in 1896, they founded the National Association of Colored Women. They could build on their history of exceptional women who boldly confronted the entrenched walls of small-minded traditions of their times. .

Though these women were prominent African-American suffragists, the movement for women's votes was fought by many lesser- known heroines. Daisy Lampkin spoke for suffrage on street corners in Pittsburg, and served on the Colored Voters' Division of the Republican National Committee. Francis Ellen Watkins Harper a suffragist sympathizer, also in 1858, refused to ride in the "colored section" of a segregated trolley car, 100 years before Rosa Parks did likewise. Mary Ann Shad Cary advocated for suffrage and many black issues. Cary as a member of the NASWA was a colleague of Susan B. Anthony and Elizabeth Cady Stanton. She graduated at age 60 from Howard University as the second African-American Lawyer in history.

Black suffragists, though often unfairly treated, maintained their integrity and recognized themselves as beneficiaries of the movement for women's equality. Unfortunately, it was the Northern black women who voted; until the 1960's southern states managed to erect barriers to prevent all black, male and female enfranchisement. Unfortunately, to this day, in some southern places, the fight for a black citizen's right to vote persists. Agitation on the part of the defeated Republican Party's candidate for president, resulted in the curtailing of some southern states' practices which had enhanced minority participation.

Ironically, though, after the long 72 years of suffragists' picketing and prison, train rides and hunger strikes, it was a lone man whose single vote passed the 19th Amendment. With an "Aye, " delivered in one soft word, young Harry Burn, the Representative from anti-suffrage Mouse Creek, Tennessee, created history. He was responding to the plea expressed in the note, hidden in his pocket.

What exactly was in that letter in Harry Burn's pocket?

It read like this: *Dear Son, Harrah and vote for suffrage. Don't keep them in doubt...Your Mother.*

Febb Burn, a widow, with a farm to run and no equal rights, knew injustice first hand. So, in the very last, final analysis, it was a single woman behind her loyal son who won Tennessee and suffrage, a lady/pawn playing smart on the landscape/board of life.

## THE ONLY WAY IS UP

# 7

# WOMEN IN A MAN'S WORLD

Much thought has been given to explain the predominance of men in the upper echelons of chess achievement. Explanations vary ; serious voices present assorted explanations. These responses diverge as laid out in *Chess News*, in a publication of the study by Robert Howard, *Personality and Individual Differences*.[12] At one extreme a comment claimed "Male predominance in chess and other sports, ...is best explained by their physical and mental superiority...Men excel in analytical and calculative fields thanks to their much better cerebral activity." [13]

A commentator "Perfect Conscience" disagreed "... connection to Math/Physics/Engineering is misguided. Many women are world leaders in these fields, and women have won Nobel Prizes. I think chess is different because it needs a certain single-mindedness to excel, something which comes more naturally to men.

Commentator Peter B took issue: Men are not more intelligent, it just that chess suits us better. Women raised in an atmosphere where this single-mindedness was encouraged - i.e., the famous Polgar sisters - have excelled

---

[12] Howard, R.W. *Explaining Male Predominance inn*, Chess News, 6/19/
[13] PerfectConscience, 6/20/2014 05:54

too."[14]

Howard also presents more, an even less sanguine view "Chess talent may consist of a mix of ability and personality traits at which males on average may excel or there may be more males at the top extreme due to greater male variability and competitiveness. Stars in chess and in physical sports often have the famed "killer instinct", the desire to win at all costs." [15]

The contention is that Chess is a "war game" and that men have a natural affinity for violence, misses the message inherent in the game. Without the element of chance, without the role of the dice or the lay of the hand, chess uses its pieces solely as a cerebral exercise, the setting happens to be military.

A salient feature of Robert Howard's study is his thesis that the disparity in performance may be due to the fact that of women's lack of participation in the highest levels of competition. Males predominate at the top in chess. Almost all grandmasters are male, there never has been a female world champion and only one female, Judit Polgar, ever has reached the top ten in the FIDE rating list (eighth spot in 2005 with a peak rating of 2735.)

The other interpretation problem is that many fewer women play chess. Look at the playing hall at an open tournament and the usual severe under-representation of women becomes apparent. In January 2012, only about 8.51% of FIDE-rated players were female. The "participation rate hypothesis" proposed by some researchers holds that the sex difference at the top in chess arises simply because so many more males play and statistically there are likely to be fewer females at the top due to their under-representation.[16]

Jacquie Van Santen presents a more practical explanation of the issue. "However, I suspect it might be in many cases that women just don't get obsessed with things like men do. They don't want to spend all their waking hours studying chess and competing hard.[17] Are women simply more versatile than their male counterparts, and better equipped to enjoy life?

However, some women shattered the stereotype. The name of the first woman who challenged the men in chess was Vera Menchik,, Russian born, British/Czech chess player, and her rise to fame in the deeply patriarchal 1920s-1930s was in many ways even more astounding than that of the fictional Beth Harmon in 1950s-1960s.[18]

---

[14] **Peter B** 6/20/2014 05:36

[15] Ibid, Howard

[16] Ibid, Howard

[17] Van Santen,Jacquie  ABC Science, *Men are Better at Chess*, June 1, 2005

[18] Chess com

*The participants of the 1929 Carlsbad tournament. Notice the separation between Vera Menchik and the rest of the players.*

Playing in more than three dozen male tournaments, Menchik continued to beat many of the top players, though she had trouble with the super-elite Russians. Still, her achievements were remarkable. "Menchik has achieved something that was unthinkable at the time — challenging the best men players of the time in chess who is "all but forgotten today."[19]

Her early death was tragic. On June 26, 1944, there was a Nazi air raid on London. Vera was residing with her mother and sister in a London suburb. During the assault, their home was hit with rocket fire. All were killed instantly. Vera was 38, a break through chess luminary's career sadly terminated.

The first U.S. woman to become a USCF Master, Gisela Gresser, came to the game by chance. Over 30, an advanced age for a chess beginner, while on a liner crossing the Atlantic, she happened on a chess manual owned by a friend. Intrigued, Gisela read carefully and taught herself the game that would be her prize. To this day, with nine titles to her name, she still holds the record for the most U.S. Women's Championships.

Like other U.S. Women's Championship participants through the years, Gresser played most of her chess games against men though games at the chess clubs were open to both men and women.

---

[19] New York Times headline in 1935. (New York Times )

Like Gresser, Grandmaster Nona Gaprindashvili was an active chess player in the 1960s. The Netflix series *The Queen's Gambit* claimed that Gaprindashvili only played against women, an error that infuriated Gaprindashvili.

The first female chess grandmaster blasted drama makers for an error about her in the Netflix series *The Queen's Gambit*. Nona Gaprindashvili, women's world champion from 1962-78, is furious that the Netflix show's is incorrectly telling viewers she never competed against men.

In an exclusive interview, Nona, 79, who was shown *The Queen's Gambit* by her granddaughter, said: "I was very displeased to discover this very serious, even crude error. "When you incorporate real people in your fictional story, it's necessary you properly check the facts. When referring to her sex, the video erroneously identifies her record, "But even that's not unusual in Russia... there's Nona Gaprindashvili... she's the female world champion and has never faced men."[20]

In fact, Nona played some of the greatest male players of all time, including at the prestigious Hastings tournament in the 1960s. Nona said she played men regularly from 1963 onwards, including Svetozar Gligoric, Paul Keres, Boris Spassky, Bojan Kurajica and Mikhail Tal. In fact, though, men seemed to find it difficult to play against a woman, Nona assumed they were afraid they might lose to a woman and suffer a loss to their prestige.

And as she said, men seemed to find it difficult to play a woman. Nona said: "Every man I ever played, especially in my early years, was hesitant to draw with me, which they'd have done against a male counterpart in an instant, because they were ashamed of losing against a woman. Mikhail Tal was a fun one." Is there a double standard in chess also? Facing a female opponent at chess will always be a challenge for a man. Could this cause men to limit their play to other men?

Asked if flirting or romance blossomed in the championships, as depicted in the show, she said: "No. They were gentlemen and they were too occupied with what happened on the board, trying to defeat me, to go for such silly shenanigans."[21]

---

[20] The Queens Gambit
[21] Newsbreak App

Nona Gaprindashvili, playing a simultaneous event against 28 men on January 11, 1965 in Dorset, England (Woods/Daily Express/Hutton Archive/Getty Images

More than 50 years since her first title win, Gaprindashvili's legacy continues. The six-time World Women's Senior Chess Champion has the main Tbilisi Chess Palace named after her. There is even a dedicated Nona Gaprindashvili Cup, awarded by FIDE, the international chess organization. The cup is unique in that it is awarded to the country with the highest combined total points across both male and female players.

Meanwhile, Gaprindashvili hopes that shows like *The Queen's Gambit* will continue to raise chess' profile. "I hope the series will bring more attention and interest in chess, just as my first victories did back in the day," she says. "Most importantly, for anyone just getting started, it is crucial to dedicate yourself as much as you can and to not back down when you face difficulties as this is a complex game. It requires a lot of attention."[22]

The political convulsions of the 1980's influenced the emigration of talented Eastern European players, men and women, to the US. Among this group was the chess phenomenon, Hungarian Zsuzsa, (Susan) eldest of the famed Polgar sisters. whose most prominent member, Judit, is considered to be the greatest female chess player in history. She is the only woman ranked in the top 10 worldwide, the Queen of Chess. They tended to compete in open tournaments, avoiding the women's championship.

Along with their third sister, Zsofia (Sofia) the Polgar siblings were conditioned by their educational psychologist father, Laszlo Polgar, to be chess marvels, because he fervently believed that "geniuses were made, not born." Home schooled, the girls were immersed in Russian, English, high level math, and especially chess, developing into amazing prodigies. Susan,

---

[22] Ibid, Newsbreak App

age 4, beat veteran players in the Budapest Chess Club. Just edging out Bobby Fisher, in December 1991, Judith achieved the Grandmaster Title, at the time the youngest ever, at 15 years, 5 months. Judith's subsequent chess life and its success, was impacted by her role as a mother when she took time off to raise her two children and saw her ratings slip. Her response might illuminate the question of male dominance in the game. "Chess is my profession and of course I hope to improve. But I'm not going to give up everything to become world champion. I have my life."[23]

Could her response speak to the heart of the matter? Would Bobby Fisher have abandoned his quest for world chess mastery in order to raise little Bobbies or Robertas? Could we ascribe women's absence in competitive chess to that pesky maternal instinct? Or might some highly talented women view chess as a compelling pastime rather than a life's single vocation.

This debate may continue or it may simply fade into irrelevancy. Surrounded by men, half of whom are hostile, the Chess Queen learned to survive and to be aggressive in a man's world of the chessboard. An illustrative parallel exists of women elected to Congress. While Chessbase sets out the arguments, women had simply proceeded to achieve as early as the '60's.

Let's take U.S. House of Representatives Speaker Nancy Pelosi for example, the most important piece on the House board. It was her "power", her Chess Queen's ability to maneuver that had her elected in a male dominated Democratic Party.

In her own words: " This is a historic moment—for the Congress, and for the women of this country. It is a moment for which we have waited more than 200 years. Never losing faith, we waited through the many years of struggle to achieve our rights. But women weren't just waiting; women were working. Never losing faith, we worked to redeem the promise of America, that all men and women are created equal. For our daughters and granddaughters, today, we have broken the marble ceiling. For our daughters and our granddaughters, the sky is the limit, anything is possible for them."[24]

*The Washington Post* political writer Paul Kane called Pelosi the most powerful House Speaker in at least 25 years, noting that some historians were comparing her influence to that of former Speaker Sam Rayburn.[25] He holds

---

[23] Allott, Serena (16 January 2002). "Queen takes all". London: Telegraph Media Group Limited. Retrieved 25 April 2010.

[24] *"Text of Nancy Pelosi's speech"*. January 4, 2007. Archived from the original on September 30, 2019. Retrieved January 19, 2019.

[25] Kane, Paul (January 11, 2020). "Showdown over Trump impeachment trial underscores power of Pelosi and McConnell". The Washington Post. Archived from the original on January 14, 2021. Retrieved January 22, 2020.

the record for the longest tenure as Speaker of the United States House of Representatives, serving for over 17 years (among his three separate stints.) Rayburn's enormous influence is set in cement, literally, in the Rayburn Office Building, located close to business in the United States Capitol Complex, South Capitol and First Street, SW.

It's too late for the Pelosi Office Building's construction; the DC real estate is all spoken for. But as a brilliant role model for politically minded women, she can take pride in the 117th Congress's record number of women participants. Women make up just over a quarter of all members of the 117th Congress – the highest percentage in U.S. history and a considerable increase from where things stood even a decade ago. A record 121 women are serving in the newly elected House, accounting for 27% of the total. In the Senate, women hold 24 of 100 seats, one fewer than the record number of seats they held in the last Congress.[26]

The Chess Queen must navigate a board full of men. It is likewise in the halls of the US Congress where 146 Congresswomen legislate with 389 men. But in a potentially tied 117th Congress' Senate vote, it is a woman, an African-American/East Asian-American, Kamala Harris who wears the crown, the ultimate deciding vote.

The Chess Queen's power is affirmed.

---

[26] Pew Research Center, "A Record Number of Women are Serving in the 117th Congress"

# NESTING QUEENS EMERGE

# 8

# THE QUEEN EVOLVES

Women's Chess received a dubious boost for all the wrong reasons with the arrival of two contenders whose remarkable beauty was a distraction from their purpose. Lisa Lane, in 1962, the second highest ranked player, the U.S. Women's Champion, caught the fancy of the chess averse press not for her talents, but for her fiery temper and enormous good looks. The cover of **Sports Illustrated**, August 8, 1961 displays chess pieces as props against her provocative gaze. Close scrutiny reveals the pieces as decidedly male: two kings and a knight. No queen need apply.

A second chess star emerged in games in New York City's Washington Square Park and the parallels between Beth Harmon in the *Queen's Gambit* and the life and times of Diana Lanni, have been described as more than coincidental, uncanny at least. At one point while playing tough chess and scoring cocaine in the City's chess scene, she shared space with Walter Tevis, the *Queen's Gambit* author. Being beautiful and flamboyant, she was most likely the prototype for Tevis' troubled protagonist. In an amazingly candid 2020 pod cast interview with Jennifer Shahade,[27] Diana details her drug

---

[27] https//thepokergrid.com2020/12/24the-grid-051-bonus-episode-ft-diana-lanni/

addiction and the wild tournament parties as portrayed by Tevis in his book, and the highly popular Netflix series, boosting her probability as the source of Tevis' character. With Tevis gone, ( died, August 8, 1984) we'll always wonder.

Rachel Crotto, emerged as the first adolescent girl of American chess, playing in the U.S. Championship at age 12. From the age of 16, when she ran away from home, she tried to make a living from tournament chess. The money challenge continued when she and her good friend, Ivona Jesierska, spent years together playing blitz chess at Barpoint, (the chess club in Manhattan also frequented by Diana Lanni,) while struggling to pay the rent. With a piece of bad advice, she was told by a radio show host to "dress very sexy, wear a low neckline, and put on a lot of makeup to use her femininity" against the condensation she perceived from the men who populated the male-dominated Open Chess Tournaments. Rachel, a lesbian, simply rejected the counsel. She was openly gay and wanted to concentrate on the game, a combination she found difficult to connect, since her sexuality drew unwanted attention. In 1986, at a Chess Olympiad in Dubai, Rachel quit the game finally; Ivona supports the duo now as a chess coordinator and coach, and they pay the rent.

So, the early 1970's saw the Chess Queen relocate. She glided with grace clear across the continent, as the Women's Chess center shifted west from New York City to California. Diane Savereide, 5-time US Champion, headed up a cadre of women chess players at UCLA. Diane specialized in Literature with a specific concentration in Russian Lit. She incorporated her Russian skills to study chess, most valuable in contests against Russian saturated competition in the interzonal in Tbilisi and other international tournaments.

An odd situation occurred in the game between Diane Savereide and England's champion, Jana Harston. According to International Master William Martz, it had been announced at the start that the rule governing one's responsibility to record one's moves would be strictly enforced. An unspecified Israeli player had even forfeited a game for refusing to record the moves under time-pressure. In the Harston-Savereide game Harston, in time pressure, stopped writing down on move 34, but Savereide (who was thought to have had an equal or better position but was also in time trouble) continued recording her moves with the impression that the arbiter would intervene. Isaac Kashdan, the chief judge, chose to let it slide, in effect giving Harston a time advantage where little time remained and which most likely was a factor in her blunder on move 39. In the appeal, it was determined that the judge had the right of discretion in this matter. It's highly probable that the lack of consistent enforcement of this rule cost Savereide either the game or a draw.

Undeterred Diane persisted playing, and brought a "modern" response to the game for women, as a full-time occupation worthy of total dedication. In her 2006 book, *Chess Bitch* Jennifer Shahade, herself a U.S. women's chess champion, narrated the following about Ms. Savereide: "Nearing thirty, with seven national titles under her belt, Diane tried to make a go as a professional player. In the summer of 1984, she took time off from her job as a computer programmer to play in tournaments, but didn't make enough money. She quit. "It came down to being thirty and I had to make a living."...For becoming the best female player in the nation, Diane would get somewhere between $300. and $600. "[28]

Again, moving east to west, the political convulsions of the 1980's influenced the emigration to the U.S. of talented Eastern European players, both men and women. Among this group was the above-mentioned chess phenomena, the Polgar sisters. Zsuzsa (Susan) eldest of the famed Hungarian Polgar sisters, 2nd, Sofia whose chess skills would surpass any normal chess player, but unfortunately, was mostly overshadowed by her two sisters. The family's most legendary member, the youngest, Judit, rounds out the Polgars' renown, and is considered to be the greatest female chess player in history, the only woman ranked in the top 10 worldwide, the Queen of Chess.

Another émigré, Irina Krush, born In Ukraine, grew up in America in Sheepshead Bay, Brooklyn, where she often went to Asser Levy Park at Coney Island and beat the men playing chess there, crafty old fellows, made tough by life in the Soviet Union. Irina recalls "I was so small I would sit on my feet so I could reach my opponent' pieces.' She also reached their hearts even though she demolished them on the board.

Irina's prodigious skills continued to mature, and at the age of 14 she won the 1998 Chess Championship to become the youngest U.S. Woman's Champion ever, and she went from there to 20 years of success. Irina Krush became one of the brightest stars of American chess, attaining the title of Grandmaster and competing internationally. Until, the stalwart competitor was attacked by a virus. In March, 2020 she was hospitalized and treated for a covid-19 infection.

She was hospitalized and treated for a "moderate" COVID-19 infection, then released to recover under quarantine at home. While quarantined, she competed in the Isolated Queens Swiss, an online women's blitz chess tournament played by internet streaming.

On March 22, though, she developed more severe breathing problems that left her in agony. She could barely sleep, and could do so only when sitting upright to alleviate the pain in her chest, calming herself with discipline hard earned on the chessboard. "It's not just a disease," she said. "It's a life trial. Chess players know what it's like to be in a bad position, to suffer. I realized it was going to be a long game, with no easy victory."[29]

---

[28] Shahade, Jennifer, *Chess Bitch*. Los Angeles: Siles Press, 2005
[29] New York Times, May 27, 2020 Waldstein, David

In April, when the Online Nations Cup was announced, Krush joined eagerly, even though she still felt lingering effects of Covid-19. Because Krush had been devoting more time to teaching than competing, many thought she would be the weak spot in the U.S. roster. The margin for error was thin. If her team was to advance, Krush could not lose the majority of her games. Things did not start well. Krush lost her first game on May 5 and, worse, immediately went back to the urgent care center, reporting more chest pain. But as her health improved, so did her chess. She played nine games over all, six of them ending in a draw, one with a victory. Though the results may sound modest, they were exactly what the U.S. team needed.

Helping her country advance to the final against China was immensely satisfying for Krush, whose final game ended in a draw against Hou Yifan, the four-time women's world champion.[30]

A story is told of Krush's opponent Hou Yifan. This unassuming Grandmaster, when just a little one, age 3 they say, her father bought for her the pretty glass chess pieces she so admired. Then he taught her the game, and, still 3, she beat him at the game. She didn't stop there. One of the current 37 women Grandmasters, in 2006, at the age of 12, Hou Yifan participated in her first Women's World Championship, reaching round 3 of the 64-player knockout tournament. Four years later, she would become the youngest-ever women's world champion.

Her accomplishments pile atop one another: she is also the youngest-ever female player to get a GM title, the youngest-ever Chinese women's champion and one of only three female players to have joined the top 100 of the world ranking — legends Maia Chiburdanidze and Judit Polgar are the other two.

In 2012, Hou chose to attend Peking University, one of China's top universities, to study international relations. It was an unusual move for a rising chess star; most forgo higher education to train and compete full time. Her coach strongly disagreed with the decision. "Use your best years for chess," he told her. "Improve as much as you can." For Hou, the choice was about forging a life beyond chess. "I want my life to be rich and colorful, not narrow," she said. "I knew it would impact my chess, but that's how I wanted to live my life."[31]

Later she won a Rhodes Scholarship at the Blayatnik School of Government, switched hats and at the 50th edition of the Biel Tournament in 2017 — she finished ahead of three 2700+ players, considered by some as her most prestigious accomplishment.

Hou Yifan, might disagree. A few days , on July 10, she broke yet another record, by becoming the youngest full professor in the history of the

---

[30] Ibid
[C]ChessBase, Chess News, 9/12/2017

University of Shenzhen, Education + Chess = full life.

An American born (Philadelphia, PA) chess talent burst on the scene with the arrival of Jennifer Shahade, a multi-talented player whose energy and ingenuity has refashioned modern chess. Where to begin? For starters we can look at her record as the two-time United States Women's Champion and her FIDE Grandmaster Title. Moving right along, we discover Jennifer, the author of *Chess Bitch*,[32] and *Play Like a Girl* where she treats us to her first hand experiences with the prominent, and often colorful chess competitors.

Dedicated players or just wannabee types can tap into her enormous supply of great ideas. Just tune into the Madwoman's Book Club, a forum for adult women (18+) to socialize over a book related to chess or to intellectual discovery. No technical chess knowledge is required. **The Madwoman's Book Club | US Chess.org**

But that's just the beginning. In 2007 Shahade co-founded a chess non-profit called **9 Queens**, a group dedicated to empowering women and at-risk youth through chess, the notion behind its name is the aspirational arrival of 8 pawns having been promoted to queens, theoretical paths to success for at-risk girls. Search @9Queens on Facebook

A poker player, in 2014, Jennifer became the Mind Sports Ambassador for PokerStars. On December 9, 2014, she won the first TonyBet Open Face Chinese Poker Live World Championship High Roller Event taking home a tidy €100,000.

Shahade hosts the lively chess podcast, "*Ladies Knight*," with pods covering varied topics, from her informed response to **The Queen's Gambit (11/19/20)** to conversations with international chess champions, Indonesian Irene Kharisma Sukandar (4/20/21.) and Women International Master, author and entrepreneur Sabrina Chevannes (2/16/21.) Shahade is also the host of the poker podcast the GRID, which she produces with her husband Daniel Meirom. In 2019, the GRID won the Global Poker Award for Podcast of the Year

Jennifer Shahade is a board member of the World Chess Hall of Fame, and directs the US Chess Women's Program at US Chess, which brings chess programming to thousands of girls all over the country.

Small wonder that chess is emerging as a popular pastime fueled by the ingenuity and dedication of chess champions like Jennifer Shahade. She has set the pace, and women, young and not so, are lacing up their running chess shoes.

---

[32] Shahade, Jennifer, *Chess Bitch.*

# *YOUNG CHESS QUEENS PARTY!*

# 9

# GEN Z 1997-2015... AND BEYOND

The Chess Queen is 1600 years young now and she's enjoying a new life of freedom and influence. Her potency on the chessboard has been long established, so now she's making her face available beyond the board. These Chess Queens reside in the latest wrinkle in social classifications, Gen Z Their generation has been distinguished by a global pandemic and by political turmoil.

These Post Millennials/Generation Z were between ages 12 and 27 during the 2008 election, where the force of the youth vote became part of the political conversation and helped elect the first black president.

Members of Gen Z are on track to be the most well-educated generation yet. These Post-Millennial women are showing major strides in college enrollment. In 2017, 64% of women ages 18 to 20 who were no longer in high school were enrolled in college.[33]

Added to that is the fact that although Millennials were the most racially and ethnically diverse adult generation in the nation's history, the *next* generation – Generation Z – is even more diverse and altered. They entered into a world permanently transformed by technology. But the same technology actually mitigated the effects of covid isolation and lack of across the board Chess. Websites such as Chess.com hosts myriad chances to play and/or to compete, to be instructed or to solve puzzles. It's all for free and easily adaptable, to the generation with little or no memory of the world as it existed before smartphones. To complete the prospects to enhance their success, Gen Z has been and continues to be inspired and groomed by the presence of savvy Millennials.

This perfect storm has fashioned our newest Chess Queens in a delightful array.

Phiona Mutesi just slipped under the wire for Gen Z, but she represents it well. Even for a generation accustomed to surprise, her story, as told in Tim Crowther's *The Queen of Katwe* [34] and a likewise named Disney film, continues to astound. The arc of her life, from a slum street kid to college student speaks to the power of chess to transform.

A meal was never guaranteed in Katwe, her home in Kampala, Uganda's worst slum. To buy food, from age 5, Phiona would hawk maize through the streets. Sometimes hungry slum kids would steal the money she had made from selling maize. Often Harriet, her mother, had to choose between rent and food and without enough money for school fees, her children rarely finished a semester.

Robert Katende, a war refugee turned missionary, had a plan for slum kids. Boys were enticed to his Sport Outreach Program's soccer games then offered porridge and an introduction to the game of chess. His notion was that the discipline and mental challenge of the game would help to prepare these kids for their problematic futures.

She was nine when Phiona trailed her brother Brian one evening, to the dusty veranda where some kids were sitting at opposites across chess boards. Katende welcomed her and assigned her an instructor, four-year-old Gloria Nansubuga. Intrigued, she then returned faithfully thereafter, learning and excelling quickly till finally the lure of the game equaled the prospect of porridge. Phiona's hardscrabble live in Katwe had preconditioned her for the contest, and by the age of eleven, she was Uganda's Junior Champion and fifteen, the national champion.

With talent too big to be confined to Uganda, Phiona's opportunity opened to the 2009 International Children's Chess Tournament in Sudan and

---

[33] Pew Research Center
[34] Crothers, Tim, *Queen of Katwe* (New York :Scribner 2012)

the 2010 Chess Olympiad in Russia. Following her performance at International Olympiads Dr. Charles Castleberry, President of Northwestern University in Kirkland, WA was inspired to offer her a scholarship He also extended the same opportunity to her Ugandan teammate, Benjamin Mukumbya. With two strong players approaching Master ratings, Dr. Castleberry decided it would be possible for the University to compete in world-class intercollegiate tournaments.

Heads turned when the Northwest University Intercollegiate Chess Team, led by college chess star Phiona Mutesi (better known as the "Queen of Katwe"), arrived at this year's Pan-American Intercollegiate Chess Championships. The attention moved to center stage when the Northwest University chess club won the trophy for the Top Small College Team category in its first season of competition.[35]

For Phiona Mutesi, the promoted Queen of Katwe, the horizon that lies beyond her newly opened door stretches far beyond the mean borders of Katwe. As her vision continues to expand, she explains herself.

"I don't feel like I really have love for chess like the way I used to have," she says. "Because, during that time, I felt like chess was all I had to use in my life. But, right now, I feel like there are a lot of stuff that I can do in my life. I feel like chess has opened the door for me.[36] More than anyone, Phiona Mutesi knows about the challenges lying behind that door, and the Queen of Katwe is prepped and ready to meet them.

Young chess champion WFM Ellen Wang geared up with her friends for the 2nd Unruly Queens chess tournament

The 21st Century's Gen Z has performed well, while all under the 19- year-old maximum age; one outstanding member is Carissa Yip at 16, the youngest female player to defeat a Grandmaster. Added to her accolades is the fact that she is the youngest American in history to become an international master.

Carissa started early, age 6, in Boston, Mass. when her father taught her, to play the game. Six months later she was able to beat him. She went on from there to winning over a Grandmaster Alexander Ivanov at age 10, the youngest female chess player to ever do that. A string of successes brought her to her latest triumph a second place in the Women's Chess Championship, a half point behind the redoubtable Irina Krush.

With opportunities for the viewer to "play" in the St. Louis 2020 Cairns Cup match, Emanuel Lasker narrates the match in which Carissa, at 17, the youngest participant. defeats the reigning women's world Champion, Ju Wenjun. [37] He pauses the video periodically to allow the viewer to enter into

[35] Northwest University Blog, December 30, 2017
[36] WBUR January 11. 2019
[37] Youtube "Deadly Stare, Deadly Game

the match, a remarkable chance to outthink the world's best players.

Meanwhile, back at her high school, Phillips Academy in Andover, Massachusetts, Carissa opened up in an interview with fellow students[38] in which she explains that she had taken a Gap Year, to pursue her International Master title, as the youngest female ever to do so successfully. She'll be busy also as having been chosen for one of the highest national honors attainable by a young chess player, to be named as a member of the 2021 All American Chess Team, just one of two females in a field of 41 males. Clarissa qualified for the age16 year group. (Look out for Alice Lee, playing strong in the 10 and under division.)

Graduating Phillips in 2022, Carissa is encouraged by the growing popularity of Chess and the lucrative opportunities in tournament prizes and chess instruction. She plans to pursue competitive chess as a career, so it's only just beginning for Clarissa Yip.

Carissa, in Conversation with Jennifer Shahade, May 19, 2020 Podcast, *US Chess Ladies Knight*, [39] Spoke of her collaboration with Jennifer Yu, a Woman Grandmaster, to respond to the pandemic with their *Chess for Covid 19* initiative. Carissa explained that it is a charity event with no entry fee, an open tournament designed to spread awareness through creating chess streaming content (CAC) *Chess.comclub/chess-*. Hoping to utilize her platform for good, Yip will donate one-hundred percent of contributions to *Direct Relief*, a foundation which provides medical resources to hospitals all around the nation.

Her fellow Grandmaster, Jennifer Yu, won the U.S. Women's Chess Championship and therefore qualified to play in the Women's World Cup.[10] She won nine games out of eleven and drew two, with Annie Wang and Tatev Abrahamyan in rounds 5 and 9 respectively. Before round 10, Yu led by 2 points ahead of the rest of the field. Because of this, nobody else in the field would be able to catch up to her for first, except for Anna Zatonskih. In the penultimate round, Yu beat her, securing the champion title with a round to spare. Yu also won the last game, finishing the tournament with a score of 10/11 points and a performance rating of 2678.

National Public Radio's Kojo Nnamdi interviewed Jennifer Yu in 2019, the U.S. Women's Chess Champion who had qualified to play in the Women's World Cup, and won the tournament with a score of 10/11 points. In a wide ranging conversation Jennifer gave an informed opinion on the popular, **The Queen's Gambit** and the aspects of playing against a computer.

---

[38] You Tube The Phillipian February 24, 2020
[39] US Chess Ladies Knight, May 19, 1920

**NNAMDI:** Jennifer, what did you think of The Queen's Gambit, and did the chess they play there ring true to a chess champion like yourself?

**YU:** I personally loved the show a lot. I thought it displayed -- like Maggie said, it just kind of showed the chess world in a pretty accurate way. It's not completely perfect, but I think it's the closest that it can be. The chess that they played on the screen was actually very accurate, which is surprising, because usually, in these kinds of movies, there's always a little bit kind of like moving magic going on, and the chess isn't very realistic.

**YU:** But I believe that they actually have two Grandmasters that were chess consultants, and that kind of showed on the screen. So, like, for example, in that clip that you just played, it's not the most accurate because, for example, in a tournament, you wouldn't really talk to your opponent at all. It's not really allowed. But, I mean, it's mainly for dramatic purposes, I believe, but these kinds of moments don't really happen in real life. But I think that they did a very good job in portraying it on the screen.

**NNAMDI:** How is it different when you're playing online from when you're playing over the board?

**YU:** It feels like a different game, to be honest, because online, you don't really see your opponent in front of you. And a lot of chess is psychological, so that kind of changes that aspect, because you're just playing on a screen. And there's also some things that you can do online that you can't do over the board. For example, online, you're allowed to do this thing called pre-moving, where you make your move before your opponent makes their move. So, it's kind of like guessing which move they make. And then it's very important when you're low on time. And online games are usually faster than over-the-board games.[40]

---

[40] Kojo Nnamdi Show, National Public Radio, February 2. 2021

So. is virtual chess yet another unintended consequence of the Covid virus? Chess, the immortal game is not only proving its immortality, but it's also showing off its agility. The Chess Queen dances, so happy to be alive!

# 10

# SOME ANSWERS AND SOME QUESTIONS

## Why Tournaments?

Our Chess Queen has always been more than a piece. As she grew and emerged through her history, she applied her power strategically and intellectually because the game's demands develop a myriad of mental skills, a not necessarily unintended benefit. To simply enjoy the game with its challenge, and cash in on these social and cerebral gifts, Chess.com offers opportunities for all players, at all levels, beginner to expert, to engage in the game.

Some Chess Queens move on to enjoy a more aggressive game plan, and an opportunity to earn a living. Yesterday's, and today's Chess Queens can compete fiercely across the board in tournaments, then stop to help or teach or learn. There are two basic types of gender specific tournaments: women's and mixed. Open tournaments are gender neutral, though for a variety of reasons, they are male dominated.

## Is there a need for girl's or women's tournaments?

Susan Polgar, probably one of the greatest woman chess players, shares her prodigious chess expertise as – Head Coach of the #1 ranked Division I team for 9 consecutive years (Webster University 2012-2021) She answers that perennial question with a first- hand response.

"This is probably one of the top 5 questions I have most often been asked over the past 15 years, since creating Susan Polgar Foundation in 2002, "[41] Susan Polgar is certainly in a position to address this question, having initially restricted her play to open tournaments. She concedes that many women were bullied verbally and emotionally, by some male chess players.

Susan goes on to clarify her response to the male vs female quandary. " I would like to walk you through some history and then explain to you some challenges girls / women face in chess. But before we start down this journey, I want to make one thing abundantly clear. I have not changed my point of view. I do strongly believe that if given equal opportunities, women are just as capable in chess, and many other STEM fields, as are men. However, I still adamantly believe that there is a serious need for **SOME** "girls only" or "women only" events.

It was my dream to revolutionize chess for young people, especially girls. I believe with all my heart that chess can and will help children of all ages, in many different aspects. Naturally, some will want to take chess seriously, maybe to become grandmasters, or even World or Olympiad Champions. But for most, chess will be a fun game which can teach them many valuable life lessons. This is important to me."[42]

[41] Chess Daily News by Susan Polgar, *Chessdailynews.com*
[42] Ibid Chess Daily News

She explains herself. "Chess is in many ways like life itself. It's all condensed in a playful manner in a game format and it's extremely fascinating because first of all I'm in control of my own destiny, I'm in charge. You have to be responsible for your actions, you make a move, you had better think ahead about what's going to happen, not after it happens, because then it's too late. Chess teaches discipline from a very early age. It teaches you to have a plan and to plan ahead. If you do that, you'll be rewarded; if you break the rules, you will get punished in life and in chess. You need to learn the rules to break the rules."[43]

GM Susan Polgar, winner of 4 Women's World Chess Championships and one of the first women in history to break the gender barrier in chess, plans ahead with The **Susan Polgar Foundation, Inc.** a non-profit 501(c)(3) corporation supported by charitable donations. So, with her characteristic zeal and determination, Susan's dream for girls flourished into the **US Girls' Junior Championship** event. The competition showcased the 21st Century line-up of girls' talent, the top players all under age 19.

Gen Z talent performed well, all under the 19- year-old maximum age, Carissa Yip the winner in 2020 for the third consecutive year earned $3,000 for her 7.5 first place win. The remaining prize money, over $7,000 was shared according to their scores to the remaining 9 players, ranging from $2000. for second place to $316. won by each of the 3 8th place winners.

Carissa Yip, who is the youngest American Female International Master, shared with everyone her experiences in open tournaments: "I don't think there's any difference in terms of play style, but in terms of psychology, yeah." All-female and all-girl tournaments, I am very much in support of those, because it just has a sense of community."

In response to an interview for her high school newspaper, Carissa commented on the advantages of an all-girl tournament.

I remember when I was a kid, I would go to my local clubs and I would be the only girl there. I remember, when I was around eight or something, I got invited to this national girls' tournament, and made a lot of female chess friends there. That social aspect of chess is really important because I feel like if you're really passionate about something but can't make friends in that field, especially at a younger age, it can discourage you and make you quit. It has a pretty detrimental effect on the number of females who play chess.[44]

---

[43] http://www.susanpolgar.com/chess-benefits/
[44] The Phillipian, February 18, 2021

**What would happen if there was no separate world chess championship for women?**

The consequences would be both financial and catastrophic for women. Prize money allows the women to concentrate on chess. Without the separate world chess tournament, it would be much harder for the women to compete with men and make enough money to continue to compete in chess. Sponsorship money might also be lost to the chess world, as some sponsors specifically target girls' and women's chess.

Moreover, it would be a disaster. For example, Hou Yifan, is the highest ranked woman among the active chess players, and is currently ranked 75th among men and women chess players. Even that vaunted rating would not allow her to make the cut in the candidates' tournaments in the World Chess Championship cycle and the prize money and media attention associated with it. Women's presence in chess would diminish and possibly disappear altogether.

**In most sports, such as golf and tennis and others, there are separate teams and events, because men seem to have the physical advantage with greater upper body strength. But chess functions on mental acuity not muscles, so why separate tournaments and a championship exclusively for women?**

Separate tournaments for girls and women don't mean that girls and women are more or less capable than boys and men at chess. They can compete, and their numbers are growing. Based on 2019 statistics, 14.6% of US Chess members are female, and that is a new, record-high percentage. Still at this point in chess history, fewer girls and women actively participate in chess. in locales where at least 50% of the new young players are girls, their initial ratings are not lower than those of boys.[45]

This study concludes that the greater number of men at the highest levels in chess can be explained by the greater number of boys who enter chess at the lowest levels.

So, with more time, this circumstance might well adjust itself...or not. Female only chess tournaments may simply coexist as they do today. Women might simply enjoy the community they create, and move on to wider ambitions.

**Where's the action for girl chess?**

The **Unruly Queens**, are totally ready to upend chess for girls. They are four young members of the US Amateur Team East 2020 who did the math and reacted when they viewed the ratio of girls to boys in chess (1:8)

These four talented young female chess players. The **Unruly Queens** consists of four girls-Martha Samadashvili, Evelyn Zhu, Yassi Ehsani and Ellen Wang- all from NY State. They grew up attending camps and playing against each other in tournaments, and later formed a team to compete in the 2020 USATE (U.S Amateur Team East) They have already increased female participation in chess by hosting free camps, tournaments, private lessons,

---

[45] Chabris, Christopher & Glickman, Mark. (2007). Sex Differences in Intellectual Performance Analysis of a Large Cohort of Co

and Q & A sessions for girls.

"We strive to create a comfortable space to empower and teach girls to play, learn and love chess. We host a number of free tournaments and camps, giving girls the opportunity to show their skills and learn from others.[46]

1. WFM Martha Samadashvili, 2019 Ruth Haring NGTOC Champion
2. WIM Evelyn Zhu, 2017 North American Under 18 Girls Champion
3. WFN Yassamin Ehsani, 2019 North American Under 18 Girls Champion
4. WFM Ellen Wang, 2017 North American Under 14 Girls Champion

They are sending out the message to all female chess players. Anyone who wants to, can be an Unruly Queen and compete hard over the chess board. In 2021 they are offering private tutoring for girls, and working on a series of group lessons. theunrulyqueens@gmail.com

The queen is the most powerful piece on the board. Although every player begins the game with only one queen, each pawn has the potential to become a queen. In theory, it is possible to transform all 8 pawns into queens, thus creating a position in which there are 9 queens on the board. One can imagine the madcap scene on the chessboard with 9 Queens, freed to dart across in straight or diagonal sorties, knights and bishops appropriately cowed. An unlikely event, but 9 Queens works as a metaphor for the capacity to empower individuals to realize their potential through chess.

***9Queens Facebook.com/9Queens*** is a 501c3, nonprofit educational organization located in Tucson, Arizona. Its mission states that 9 Queens is dedicated to empowering individuals and communities through chess by making the game fun, exciting, and accessible. We offer free chess education programs specifically designed to promote critical thinking skills, academic performance, and self-confidence. Our mission is to use chess as a tool to motivate, empower, and engage under-served and under-represented populations to realize their potential and achieve academic and personal success.[47]

---

[46] Theunrulyqueens@gmail.com
[47] 9Queens.org

### What is the Woman's World Championship Event?

The Women's World Chess Championship is played to determine each year's world champion in women's chess' tournament winner. The **2020 Women's World Chess Championship** featured Ju Wenjun world champion as winner of the 2018 knock-out championship, and her challenger, Aleksandra Goryachkina, the winner of a newly established Candidates Tournament that was held in 2019.[2]Aleksandra Goryachkina replaced Hou Yifan, who declined an invitation.[6]

The **2022 Women's World Chess Championship** is an upcoming chess match for the Women's World Chess Championship title. It is contested by the defending champion Ju Wenjun (winning the 2020 match) and her challenger, the winner of the 2021 Candidate tournament.

### How To Play In US Chess Online Rated Tournaments?

Opportunities abound to play chess online. So, whereas contact sports require presence and ballgames require venues, competitive chess can function fully on line. Its implementation is welcoming, adjusting the level of competition to the player's choice. Casual players are proliferating; chess clubs are booming. An estimated 16 million games are being played online every day since the pandemic lockdown began—9 million of them on Chess.com alone.[48]

FIDE and Chess.com combined efforts to offer the highest ever high

---

[48] Chess.com

prize money for the winner of the **2021 Women's Speed Chess Championship** an online competition for top female chess players worldwide. The main event scheduled **June 10 to July 3,** 2021 preceded by eight qualifiers from **May 28 to June 6.** Women from all continents had the chance to participate in this unique event and fight for a piece of the **$64,000** total prize fund. First place will win $20,000, With cash prizes through to the 16 place finisher.

Effective Thursday, April 15, 2021, the New York City Marshall Club, has opened in a limited capacity, to across the board events. The club is opening with tight restrictions, and is only open to vaccinated members

All online events require Zoom. Online tournaments additionally require a chess.com account. Shortly after registration is closed, registered participants will receive an email with the Zoom meeting ID and (for tournaments) the chess.com links necessary to play. Players who are late to enter chess.com for their tournament will miss the event and will not be refunded.[49]

The U.S. Congress, in May 2013 declared St. Louis, Missouri the Chess Capital of the country. The Saint Louis Chess Club, a 501(c)(3) educational organization, is the premier chess facility in the country and one of the best in the world. [50] The Chess Club offers many varied opportunities including beginner classes for kids and adults, ladies-only beginner classes and great tournament chess options for women.

Will our future years remain mostly on line? Maybe soon we will return to regular physical competition.

Theoretically over the board play will resume with tournaments also planned for European, Asian and African sites. Aspirational matches that will happen again.

One day… soon?

[49] https://www.marshallchessclub.org
[50] Stlouischessclub.org

# Chess Game Glossary

**Algebraic Notation**: the standard method for recording and describing the moves in a game of <u>chess</u>. It is based on a system of coordinates to uniquely identify each square on the chessboard. Each one of the chessboard 64 squares is assigned a letter and a number. From left to right A to H, vertically 1-8, for example The opening Queens are located on either d1 or d8

**Blindfold Chess:** Players cannot actually see the board, but play by using Algebraic Notation.

**Blitz** games typically give five to ten minutes per player, and "rapid" games give between ten and sixty minutes.)

**Castling:** A smart move that provides a safe place for a king and a get out of jail card for the rook, but only if they have never moved before, and if the king is not moving into check. These two pieces can break check rules. The king can move two places to either side and the rook can jump over the king into his adjacent space.

**Check:** When the king is under attack he must escape immediately. He might capture the attacking piece, or eliminate the attacker with another piece or he might simply move out of check.

**Checkmate:** The king is stymied; he is not in check but has no legal moves. Game over

**Draw** A **draw** occurs in **chess** when neither player wins nor loses— the game ends in a tie. Either of the two players can ask for a **draw.** Draws occur when there are insufficient pieces for either side to check or when the position is repeated three times. In tournament play a draw is worth a half point.

**Elo Rating**: Named for Arpad Elo, it is an accepted rating system for chess players based on their tournament results.

**End Game:** The final portion of the game in which pieces have been reduced and winner pretty much decided

**Fast Chess:** Fast chess is a type of chess in which each player is given less time to consider their moves than normal tournament time controls allow. Fast chess is further subdivided, by decreasing time controls, into rapid chess, blitz chess, and bullet chess. Armageddon chess is a particular variation in which different rules apply for each of the two players.

**FIDE: (Federation International Des Eches)** Recognized as the instrument of worldwide Chess. FIDE federation organizes the Chess Olympiad and the World Championship matches, the most high-status Chess tournaments

**Gambit:** A gambit (from ancient Italian gambetto, meaning "to trip") is a chess opening in which a player sacrifices material with the aim of achieving a subsequent positional advantage.

**Grandmaster, GM Grandmaster:** Awarded by FIDE it is the most prestigious title in Chess. A Grandmaster generally holds a rating of 2500 or greater. Magnus Carlsen the current World Chess Champion, World Rapid Chess Champion, and World Blitz Chess Champion has a current (May 2021) FIDE rating of 2847

**International Master IM,** The second most prestigious Chess title awarded by FIDE, generally bestowed on players with a rating of 2450 or higher.

**Master** holds a rating of over 2200.

**Material:** The game pieces and their individual point values. Pawn (1), Knight (3), Bishop (3) Rook (5), Queen (9). The king has no value, since he can't be captured. Players consider point value when evaluating possible trade off with opposing pieces.

**Middle Game:** The phase in the game between the Opening Game and the End Game. This part is where the decisive action occurs, where players must utilize strategy and creativity.

**Olympiad:** In 1924 an attempt was made to include Chess as an Olympic Sport. Though the effort failed, the first unofficial Olympiad was held that year in Paris. Since 1950 they have been held regularly every two years. Due to the pandemic, the Olympiad was held on line in 2020. Russia is scheduled to host the 2022 Olympiad.

**Open** (See Tournament Types)

**Opening:** The first phase of the game in which the pieces are developed. Players enact their openings through a memorized series of steps. One of the oldest openings still in use today is the Queen's Gambit, first mentioned in the Gottingen Manuscript in 1450. A pawn is sacrificed to enhance a p control of the center.

**Point:** A unit used to score the results of a chess game. Win-1, draw 1/2 , loss 0

**Rapid Chess (See Tournament Types)**

**Resign:** To give up by reason of inevitable checkmate or paucity of material.

**Score sheet:** All moves made by each player must be recorded as they are made.

**Skittles Room**: Room where post-game analysis is conducted

**Stalemate** Though the king not in check but a side has no legal moves or captures to be made the game cannot continue.

**Time Control:** A predetermined time limit exists for a player to complete a move. The player loses the game if limit is exceeded. Time controls vary from three minutes in a Blitz Game to three hours in a classical game.

**Tournament types**:

      **Elimination-**A single-elimination, knockout, or sudden death tournament **is a type** where the loser of each match-up is immediately eliminated from the tournament. Each winner will play another in the next round, until the final match-up, whose winner becomes the tournament champion

      **Knockout-**Event where a player is eliminated after losing a match.

      **Open-**Accepts all who apply, though generally a includes an entry fee.

      **Rapid Chess-**Games with time controls which range from 25 minutes to 60 minutes a player.

      **Round Robin-**An event in which everyone plays everyone else.

      **Simultaneous:** An event when a strong player can take on many opponents at once.

**USCSF Chess Federation:** The US Chess Federation (US Chess) is the official governing body and nonprofit 501(c)(3) organization for chess players and chess supporters in the United States.

**Woman Grandmaster WGM:** Gender specific titles awarded by FIDE to women.

**Woman International Master** WIM: See above

**Women's World Championship:** World Championship tournament in which all participants are women. A series of candidates' tournaments and matches determine the challenger who will play a head-to-head match against the title holder.

**World Championship** is a chess match between the reigning world champion and a challenger. Magnus Carlsen is the world champion in 2021,

# Appendix

## Women's Chess

**Ladies Knight, Ladiesknight.org** is the official podcast of USChess *Jennifer Shahade,* two-time US Women's Chess Champion hosts Ladies Knight a monthly podcast featuring female chess champions and leaders. The podcast debuted on January 2019. Jennifer Shahade also co -hosts with Adia Onyango the *Madwoman's Book Club.* Sessions feature a mini-chess-lesson, open forum discussion and authors, and special guests This thinking woman's book club will provide a forum for adult women (18+) to socialize over a book related to chess or intellectual discovery. No technical chess knowledge required. USChess.org/bookclub

**9 Queens**: 9Queen.org is a nonprofit educational organization dedicated to empowering individuals and communities through chess by making the game fun and accessible.

**Unruly Queens:** theunrulyqueens.wixsite.com/website strive to create a comfortable space to empower and teach girls to play, learn and love chess. The Unruly Queens host free tournaments and camps.

**USChess:** new.uschess.org/give/women-chess-initiative Recognizing that women a growing segment of the US Chess community, US Chess has responded with a multi-pronged approach to empower women and girls through chess.

A computer search will result in the names and locations of chess gatherings and clubs located in cities and state chess groups. For example:

## Some Great Places to Play Chess

### Chess and Checkers House in Central Park in New York City

Though you can play chess and checkers in almost any New York City Park, only at the Chess & Checkers House can you borrow pieces for your game. Dominoes and backgammon are also available. The 24 tables surrounding this rustic pagoda are blessed with ample shade, ideal for a chess or checkers game any time of year. If you don't have a player, the park staff will help you find one. (unfortunately closed due to the pandemic. Expected to reopen soon, though as of 5/27/21, it remained "Closed until further notice.")

## Washington Square Park , New York City
### 5th Avenue, Waverly Place

## St. Louis Chess Club 4657 Maryland Avenue St. Louis, MO
### saintlouischessclub.org

The Saint Louis Chess Club, open to the public from 12 PM to 8PM every day, not only offers a complete array of chess events and instruction, also features the Guinness World Record's certification of the World's Largest Chess Piece.

# Chess Tournaments

**USChess: USChess.org Complete listing of tournaments available by type, location and date**

# Learning Sites for Kids

**Chess Palace Chesspalace.com  Judith Polgar** "Playing chess is not the goal, it is a tool; an extremely efficient tool for logical thinking and a quick, smart decision-making. Chess Palace is a learning playground with physical boundaries of the chessboard and endless creative solutions in education."

**Chess.com** is an internet chess server, internet forum and social networking website.[3] The site has a freemium model in which some features are available for free, and others for accounts with subscriptions. Live online chess can be played against other users at daily, rapid, blitz or bullet time controls, with a number of chess variants available. Chess versus an AI, computer analysis, chess puzzles and teaching resources are also offered.

The site additionally has news articles and tournament coverage. It has hosted online tournaments including Titled Tuesdays, the PRO Chess League, the Speed Chess Championship, and computer vs computer events.

**Young Royalty Chess Academy** youngroyaltychess.com Young Royalty is dedicated to serving the community, people of color, and small business owners. Offered free chess programming at Buffalo, NY local community centers

**Chess In The Schools**
https://chessintheschools.org
 Chess in the Schools fosters the intellectual and social development of low-income youth through chess education. 500,000 students have been taught Chess in 48 New York City schools

The NSCF (National Scholastic Chess Foundation) is excited to provide chess instruction online. If you would like to enroll your child in one of our online classes, click the button to see current offerings.

If you are a school, after-care, or other organization serving children that would like to consider adding chess to your programming, contact us. We welcome new partnerships and opportunities to share the many benefits chess can provide in education and building community.

https://nscfchess.org/#https://nscfchess.org/#

## Scholastic Tournaments - Illinois Chess Association
https://il-chess.org /all-events
The Scholastic Tournament Program offers free competitive chess tournaments in New York City. Tournaments normally are hosted primarily in public schools and many are open to all New York City students. Tournament participation ranges from approximately 400-700 students. Chess in the Schools organizes and manages the tournament and through our Grand Prix initiative, also offers competitive grants to schools that participate in the School Program to be used for competing in regional and national scholastic tournaments.

**National Scholastic Chess Foundation nscfchess.org** The NSCF specializes in curricular chess instruction and offers strategic development support for schools and other partners. In New York and Connecticut, they operate programs in over 70 schools in 30 different communities. They acknowledge excellence in both chess and education through the National Scholar Chess Player awards and provide scholarships to our programs on the basis of need.

## Bibliography

### Videos
Queen of Katwe (film)
Brooklyn Castle
Bev Grant Women are coming

### Books
Norwood, David *Chess Puzzles,* London: Usborne Publishing Ltd.
Shahade, Jennifer. *Chess Bitch*. Los Angeles: Siles Press, 2005
Capablanca, Jose.*Chess Fundamentals*
Shenk, David. *The Immortal Game*. New York: Doubleday Broadway Publishing Group, 2006.
Yalom, Marilyn. *Birth of the Chess Queen*. New York: HarperCollins, 2004

## You Tube
Bev Grant Women are coming
Chess the Musical
Chess Sitzprobe
Women's Day Play Magnus Group

## Magazines
Chessbase en.chessbase.com
ChessGossip Chessgossip.com

## Chess Puzzles
Chessinvasion.com good source for trivia Questions

## Online Sources

## Women's Chess news on Twitter
@Girlbosschess
Twitter.com/girlbosschess: A collective of women chess players who look to educate and inspire women and girls.
USChessWomen Stories, Tactics featuring women and girls in the @USChess community.
The latest *Tweets* from Jennifer Shahade (@JenShahade). Author, 2x US *Women's chess* champ, @PokerStars Pro & director @USChessWomen ...
## Susan Polgar (@SusanPolgar) | Twitter
https://twitter.com › susanpolgar The latest *Tweets* from Susan Polgar (@SusanPolgar). ... ECU Girls'
and *Women's # Chess* Weekend starts tomorrow with hundreds of female participants taking ...

## Women's Chess News on Instagram
Instagram.com/uschesswomen

## Women's Chess News on You Tube
U.S. Women's Championship Match, October, 2020. St. Louis Chess Club sponsored match

:

# CHESS PUZZLE 1

*WHITE TO MOVE, WITH THE INTENT OF*
*FORCING A DRAW IN ONE MOVE*

# CHESS PUZZLE 2

*BLACK TO MOVE, WITH A CHECKMATE IN ONE MOVE*

# CHESS PUZZLE 3

*WHITE TO MOVE, FORCED CHECKMATE IN 3 MOVES*

## CHESS PUZZLE 4

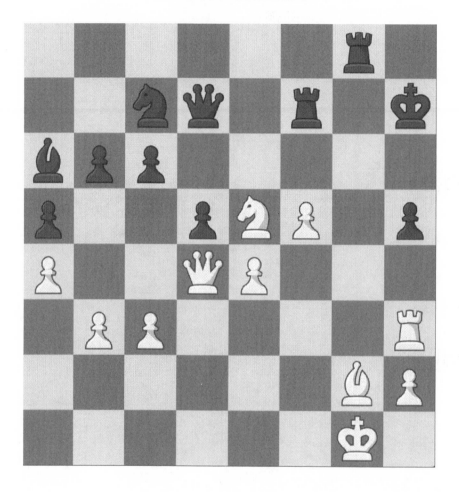

## *WHITE TO MOVE. FORCED MATE IN THREE*

# CHESS PUZZLE 5

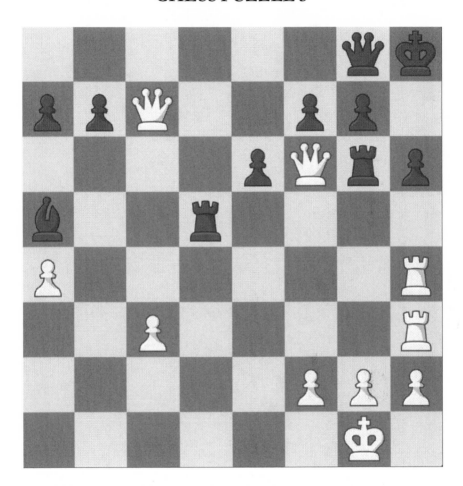

## *WHITE TO MOVE WITH A FORCED CHECKMATE IN 5 MOVES*

The solutions to the previous puzzles are as follows:

Chess Puzzle 1:
    1. Rg2+ Kh7 2. Rxg7 Kxg7
Chess Puzzle 2:
    1. Qg5#
Chess Puzzle 3:
    1. Qb7+ Kd6 2. Re8+ Rd7 3. Qxd7#
Chess Puzzle 4:
    1. Rxh5+ Kg7 2. Kxd7+ Rf6 3. Qxf6#
Chess Puzzle 5:
    1. Rxh6+ Rxh6 2. Rxh6+ Qh7 3. Qc8+ Rd8 4. Qfx8+ Bxd8 5. Qxd8#

During her career as an educator, Patricia Cuff, MA, continues to view historic developments through a related alternate lens. Readers with starting points parallel to the text, view history in a larger light.

She has contributed to a variety of magazines, including Scholastic Search and Washington, DC publications. She has published two books on the suffrage movement's most controversial good trouble makers, Alice Paul and Lucy Burns.

Patricia Cuff maintains an active role in today's most urgent issues, women's rights and environmental justice.

Made in the USA
Middletown, DE
22 December 2021